HOW
ARCHITECTURE WORKS

HOW
ARCHITECTURE
WORKS

Douglas E. Gordon

Stephanie Stubbs

Illustrated by Timothy B. McDonald

VNR VAN NOSTRAND REINHOLD
_____ New York

Copyright © 1991 by Van Nostrand Reinhold

Library of Congress Catalog Card Number 90-49703
ISBN 0-442-23951-3

Printed in the United States of America

Van Nostrand Reinhold
115 Fifth Avenue
New York, New York 10003

Chapman and Hall
2–6 Boundary Row
London, SE1 8HN, England

Thomas Nelson Australia
102 Dodds Street
South Melbourne 3205
Victoria, Australia

Nelson Canada
1120 Birchmount Road
Scarborough, Ontario MIK 5G4, Canada

16 15 14 13 12 11 10 9 8 7 6 5 4 3 2 1

Library of Congress Cataloging in Publication Data

Gordon, Douglas E.
    How architecture works/by Douglas E. Gordon and Stephanie Stubbs;
    illustrated by Timothy B. McDonald.
        p. cm.
    Includes bibliographical references and index.
    ISBN 0-442-23951-3
    1. Architecture. I. Stubbs, Stephanie. II. Title.
NA2520.G58 1991
    720—dc20   90-49703
                                                                   CIP

CONTENTS

FOREWORD

The authors are clearly hooked on architecture—the process, the profession, the end products. And their enthusiasm is infectious. There is no way that anyone could read this book and not come away with a new fascination with our built environment and the ways in which it is created.

This book has succeeded at a very difficult task: demystifying architecture without oversimplifying it or subjecting it to a *People* magazine kind of popularization.

This is a very accessible book, demanding of the reader no prerequisites except an inquiring mind and an appreciation of readable, even entertaining, prose. Yet behind every chapter is a great deal of sophistication. Two acute observers of architecture have distilled a storehouse of information, some of which will be new even to many practicing architects. This is particularly true of the chapter on materials, with its wonderful base of history.

The book has an unusual, even idiosyncratic, organization. Interspersed with the hard data are humanizing quotes and anecdotes. The narrative is in the form of answers to a series of 75 questions.

My advice to the reader is not to feel driven to sit down and read the book sequentially, much less at one sitting. Some questions are bound to be more interesting to you than others. I find "Who oversees construction?" more engaging than "How is dirt kept from caving in on a construction site?"

Pick the questions most compelling to you and start with them. Or read the delightful quiz at the end of the book and follow its leads to enticing morsels.

There is considerable evidence of a growing interest in architecture on the part of nonarchitects. A book like this can fan such interest, take it to new heights, and make it at once more rewarding and more enjoyable. So enjoy.

Donald Canty, Hon. AIA

Architecture is by nature of its products a serious profession. The sweat of an architect's brow is (sometimes literally) cast in stone, for all the world to see, to use, to pronounce verdict upon. Buildings tend to last a long time, and the way they look and function has profound ramifications on the people who live, work, and play in them.

But who can deny the sheer delight and satisfaction generated by a fine-tuned work of architecture? We all have our favorites—the Empire State Building, San Simeon Castle, St. Paul's Cathedral, Jefferson's Monticello, maybe Grandpa's farmhouse or the local community church. The feat of someone designing and constructing a place that feels "just right" for its intended function is so complex that it tends to be mysterious.

In our years of writing technical materials to aid architects in the practice of their profession, we have examined the "mysteries" of architecture on a brick-by-brick basis through their technologies. Most of the time, the materials and constructions used by architects have a simple, logical explanation. Sometimes the reasoning is centuries old, sometimes it is a new technology; but it is always fascinating. Our purpose in writing this book is to unravel some of the mystery in plain English, to laypeople who have been awe-inspired by a building and pondered some of its reasons to be.

One should never deny the magic behind the bricks and mortar. The architect's special gift of turning building materials into great spaces and places has not been adequately put into words, even (or especially) to the satisfaction of the architect. But one can demystify various practices of architecture, and why architects do some of the things they do.

Considering the gauntlets a person crosses just to enter this notoriously low-paid profession leads quickly to the conclusion that architects operate out of love, not money. To become a registered architect, one conquers at the very least five years of college education to earn a professional degree, a minimum of three years apprenticeship (today called an "internship," usually at "preprofessional" wages) to a registered architect, and a grueling nine-part, 32-hour examination.

By the time a person is a registered architect, he or she is a careful balance of artist and scientist who communicates in an arcane language we call "archibabble." Archibabble is three-quarters legitimate professional code/shorthand, and one-quarter voodoo. We are fluent in archibabble ourselves and use it freely in our work, but have taken pains to avoid it in this book in order to dissolve one layer of confusion for the reader.

We also have tried to avoid the ponderous sense of solemnity that seems to surround the noble art of building design in favor of its lightheartedness and joy. Everything created by humans, including architecture, has its funny side. For this reason, we begin each chapter with an architect joke that captures the tenor of the chapter. This was no easy task—one must search far and wide for architect jokes. There should be more, and perhaps there will be as the public comes to understand and appreciate what exactly architects do.

In the same spirit, we have created the "cocktail party pop quiz" at the end of the text. Architecture today, the most public of the arts, belongs as much to backyards and pizza parlors as it once did to the parlors of rich patrons and the intelligensia.

The questions themselves represent only a sampling of the many issues the architect considers during the design of a building. They are not meant in any way to encompass the whole of architectural design; only to whet the appetite for more knowledge on a particular subject. Volumes have been written on the topic of each question. For this reason, we provide a suggested readings list from which the reader can obtain further information.

Each question leads to, easily, a hundred other questions. We selected, first of all, a number of questions we hear asked most often about architecture. We added to that list some questions to which we already knew the answers, and thought were nifty clues to the architectural mystique. Finally, we threw in some questions we thought we ought to be able to answer, and learned the answers during our research. At that stage, the questions divided themselves neatly into four major areas of concern: materials, building systems, the practice of architecture, and contemporary concerns. These areas became the major chapter headings.

Like most writers, we are indebted to those who pioneered the topic preceding our own research; you will find their names cropping up again and again in our resource lists. Timothy McDonald, the illustrator of this book, captured the spirit of joy we speak of with his drawings. Trained as an architect, he believes and lives it. Forrest Wilson taught us we could do it, and Don Canty showed us how to do it right.

HOW
ARCHITECTURE
WORKS

CHAPTER ONE MATERIALS

Architects are high in credibility in spite of the often-held belief that they are bad business managers. Architects, on the whole, do the work they do not because of a quest for money, but for an inner satisfaction that comes from creative, well-thought-out, well-crafted form. And, as anyone knows who has played with building blocks, made sand castles, or built a stick house, the nature of the materials being used has a direct impact on the forms that are possible. One of the first understandings a student of architecture reaches is the fundamental importance of understanding building materials—separately, and in combination with one another.

Humans have always crafted shelter. Stone, mud, grass, saplings, wood, and dung all were common building materials long before our predecessors got around to figuring out how to record their exploits in writing. Architects still use a substantial amount of stone and wood, although in different ways from our prehistoric forebears.

The first wildly successful man-made building material was the brick. Humble and unassuming, brick is small, lightweight, basic in form, and cheap. Brick suffices when unskilled laborers need quick, durable shelter. The same material also satisfies the artistic demands of master designers and crafters. How did bricks come to be? And how do they work? For instance, why do bricklayers stack them in different patterns?

Another artificial material that is a mainstay in modern construction is concrete. In fact, we often think that concrete is a product of the twentieth century. Not so. The Romans, using all-natural cement, built concrete structures all across their empire that stretched from Great Britain to Africa. Then it disappeared from the construction scene for centuries. Not until we could manufacture cement, a nineteenth-century innovation, did concrete make its resurgence.

Iron and steel are great building materials, but they are very expensive. Before mass production they were too expensive to be used as a building material. Once enough iron and steel was available, and once someone realized it could be used as a frame, covered with other materials, steel became part of the architect's rapidly expanding palette.

And what have architects been covering their steel structures with the past decade or two? Shiny glass, of course. That's a story unto itself. Plastic, the marvel material of the modern age, has not had the success of glass as a building cladding material, though. And that's another story altogether.

Besides structure and cladding, architects need material for their roofs, they need paint to protect other materials and make the building look the way they want, and they even need material to fill the gaps between their other materials. The story of materials is the story of architecture.

How did brick come to be?

Brick represents a unique concept in building materials, because it is a transformed material, as opposed to a wood or stone that is used the way it occurs in nature and is simply reshaped. The raw materials that make up bricks have to be combined in the correct amount, shaped, and fired. Archeologists speculate that the concept of masonry building has its origins in the creation of low walls from stones or pieces of caked mud. The precursor to mortar was wet mud packed into the cracks of the wall to give it stability and weather resistance. Early mud bricks were not viewed as the greatest thing until sliced bread; stones were the building material of choice wherever they were available.

The use of brick as a building material reached its first wave of popularity during the Roman Empire.

Fires built against mud brick walls may have brought a spontaneous knowledge of the hardness and stability of burned brick, and thus led to the invention of the kiln some 10,000 years ago. Since then the popularity of bricks has been cyclical. During the Roman Empire, bricks rose to the status of popular and ubiquitous building material. By the time the Middle Ages were in full swing in Europe, bricks were more expensive than stone, and used only when stone was not available. Gradually they increased again in popularity to the point that, during the eighteenth century, they were considered a cheap substitute for stone. Today, with our options of building materials, and because of the high cost of labor (laying brick is a labor-intensive process, even in the labor-intensive construction industry), they have strong competition for their share of the market.

The major component of bricks is clay, a compound of silica and alumina, with various oxides that give the brick its color when fired. To make bricks, the clay is mixed with water, fired for a day or two at about 300 degrees Fahrenheit, and then fired again at a much higher temperature (1,600 to 2,400 degrees Fahrenheit). In addition to the oxides present in the clay, the color of the bricks produced depends on the temperature and chemistry of the fire in the kiln. For instance, higher temperatures produce darker bricks (and greater shrinkage). Iron oxide turns the bricks red in an oxidizing fire and purple in a reducing (oxygen-producing) fire. The product of fire, bricks are among the most fire resistant of materials —as evidenced by long-standing use in chimneys and kilns.

Considering the trouble that it takes to make bricks, and the fact that laying masonry is labor intensive and requires a certain level of skill and experience, why would we bother with brick construction at all? Many speculate that the fondness people feel for brick has to do with its scale and size—a brick is dimensioned to fit the human hand. There is no real "standard" brick; a designer selecting bricks for a building usually chooses from actual samples of brick runs. The rule of thumb is that three courses (horizontal rows) of brick plus the three accompanying mortar joints is equal to 8 inches high.

Brick sizes are listed in the following order: width (thickness), height, and length. The nominal size of a standard brick is 4 by 2⅔ by 8 inches. (The actual width of the brick may vary by 3/32 inch, and the length by ¼ inch, under the standards of brickmaking.) Of course, specially made bricks can be had in almost any size. Common sense and the nature of the material dictate upper and lower limits (3 by 2 by 8 inches and 8 by 8 by 16 inches).

The small scale of the brick as a unit of design gives the designer great flexibility in designing patterns and textures of walls and floors. And there is great geometric wonder in the forms of the Roman vaults, the dome of the Pantheon, and Jefferson's serpentine wall at the University of Virginia, all composed of brick.

Do different patterns of bricks mean different things?

The pattern in which bricks are laid in a wall, called a pattern bond, can give clues to the wall's structural nature or can simply be decorative. The actual size of a brick, 3⅝ inches wide by 2¼ inches high by 7⅝ inches long, has developed over the ages because it is easy (and at 8 pounds, light enough) for a mason to manipulate with one hand. The size also allows for numerous patterns, because the length (7⅝ inches) equals the width of two bricks (7²⁄₈ inches) plus a mortar joint (⅜ inch). A brick placed parallel to the face of a wall is called a *stretcher*, while a brick perpendicular to the wall face is called a *header*.

Walls that are one brick wide, called single-wythe walls, are most commonly laid in a *running bond*, in which alternating courses of bricks overlap each other by half of their width. It was especially important to do this before portland cement became an affordable ingredient in mortar, and mortars were much weaker than the brick.

If you stack bricks on top of one another, you end up with straight lines of mortar running up the wall, in which cracks could form. With today's higher-strength mortar, though, brick courses can be placed exactly on top of each other in what is called a *stack bond*. Stack bonds have a different look that can be used with striking results, but it still is not used too frequently because a stack bond is inherently weaker than a running bond.

In walls with more than one wythe, header bricks connect adjoining wythes. For instance, a double-wythe wall is as thick as two stretchers mortared together side by side, which, because of the proportions of standard brick, is the same measurement as the length of a header brick. A *common bond* wall has a full course of header bricks at every sixth course up the wall. An *English bond* wall places every other course in the header position. Again, this interlocking of stretchers and headers, important for structural strength in days of yore when mortar was weak, is not as important with today's cement-based mortars, although many designers still use them because of the way they look.

Different patterns of brick usually reflect the architect's or the mason's preference. Walls here are running bond. In the door arch, brick with their long faces showing are stretchers; the ones above, with their short faces showing are headers.

WHAT IS TERRA COTTA?

Terra cotta has been around in many shapes and forms since the time of the ancient Romans and Greeks. Often it is used to imitate other materials, from bricks to all kinds of stone. Literally meaning "burnt earth" in Italian, terra cotta in its broadest definition includes flower pots, statues, and some types of brick. It is hard-baked, fine-grained clay. Similar to common brick in makeup, it is made of a better grade of clay and fired at higher temperatures.

New York City's Woolworth Building, completed by architect Cass Gilbert in 1913, offers some fine examples of terra cotta ornament. The terra cotta is currently being replaced, piece by piece.

Terra cotta can be molded or extruded into plain or decorative shapes of moderate detail. It was quite popular from the 1890s to the 1930s for cladding and both exterior and interior decoration on major buildings, such as the Woolworth Building in New York City. Terra cotta was popular for skyscraper trimmings because it was lighter than stone. Molds could be reused, so buildings could have repetitious ornament that could be made cheaply. Most commonly, architectural terra cotta takes the form of hand-made hollow pieces, often blocks approximately 4 inches deep, measuring 12 by 18 inches, and applied to building exteriors.

Terra cotta was first used extensively in this country for rebuilding following the fire of 1871 in Chicago. Its use spread rapidly to the Midwest (St. Louis still has many fine examples), and to Boston and New York. Until 1890, most terra cotta was used in its natural, warm-brown color, often in combination with brick. It also made an inexpensive substitute for brownstone. "Brownstone" terra cotta was used unglazed for decorative panels, chimney caps, finials, and the like. For protection from the elements, it was often painted. Colored terra cotta, usually yellow, buff, or glazed white, subsequently became popular, often as an accompaniment to limestone.

The improvement of glazes, which became popular about five years later, gave rise to terra cotta in almost any color. The Art Deco period of the 1920s popularized terra cotta in black, gold, green, and peach, all requiring the application of glaze. Unglazed terra cotta found use as fireproofing and as a structural material. Hollow, machine-formed bricks were used in arches and for bearing walls. Terra cotta was also pressed into service for roofing, floor, and wall tiles.

Machine-made terra cotta, which was invented in the 1930s, is an extruded product referred to as *ceramic veneer*. It usually has a flat face and either a flat or ribbed back, and is attached to a backup wall.

Today, terra cotta as "imitation" stone, brick, or whatever is not the inexpensive solution that it was at the turn of the century. In fact, there are few manufacturers of terra cotta left in this country. Designers tend to look for materials that imitate the look of terra cotta when they have to replace portions of terra-cotta facades. "Fake" terra-cotta ornamentation is popularly constructed of fiberglass; precast concrete; stucco; metals (iron, steel, or aluminum); and ironically, cut stone—the material terra cotta originally imitated. Is it or isn't it a real terra-cotta facade? Sometimes, only your architect knows for sure.

How can I tell what kind of stone a building is made of?

If you studied earth science in high school, chances are that you know the three basic geological classifications of stone. Sedimentary stones often have a layered look, because they are composed of small fragments of preexisting rock that are deposited in layers by air or water. Sandstone (one common type is brownstone, found in the New York City rowhouses that bear its name), shale (which, made of clay, is too soft to be used in most building applications), and limestone (which is composed mostly of calcium carbonate) are common types of sedimentary stone. Dolomite limestone, widely used in many parts of the world, has a double carbonate of calcium and magnesium. Chalk is a soft white limestone; travertine is a form of limestone into which vegetable material is embedded.

Igneous rocks, such as pumice and granite, are created by volcanic action at the earth's surface.

Metamorphic rocks are sedimentary or igneous rocks modified by heat or pressure into a different structure. As examples, marble is metamorphic limestone, and slate is metamorphasized shale. Gneiss is metamorphasized igneous rock (such as granite) or sedimentary rock. It is known by its banded texture.

Knowledge of earth science, however, is not enough to get you around a quarry to choose stone for a building application. The building industry classifications for stone are just confusing and different enough to baffle a purist geologist. The industry chooses its own classification by performance and appearance of the stone. For instance, in the building industry, not all geological limestones are called limestones. If the type of limestone employed is capable of taking on a surface polish, it is called a marble. Granite to the building industry includes all igneous rocks and gneiss. Poor, lonesome travertine is caught in the middle—sometimes it is described as marble and sometimes as limestone.

The industry classification makes it easier to group stones in a structural way. The rule of thumb is that most granites and marbles are stronger than your average structural concrete, but many limestones (and sedimentary stones, such as sandstones) are weaker.

This kind of classification also helps group stones as to their reactions to the environment. Some types of stone, like travertine, are very soft when they are quarried, and harden (and consequently shrink in size) after they are cut. For this reason, they must be seasoned before they are cut to their final size, just like wood. Other stones are particularly sensitive to sulphur dioxide, which finds its way into the atmosphere as a by-product of many industrial processes. When sulphur dioxide combines with water, it forms sulphuric acid (the notorious "acid rain"), which can dis-

Irregularly shaped stones laid at random define a rubble pattern; rectangular blocks of stone form an ashlar pattern.

solve calcium carbonate, the main ingredient of limestones and certain sandstones.

Cracks in stone can cause severe building deterioration, particularly in climates with sudden temperature changes that cause water trapped in the cracks to freeze (and expand) and then thaw (and contract) in cycles that weaken the stone (see pp. 16–19). All stone is subject to temperature and moisture movement, and must be accommodated with expansion joints. When stones are held in place by mortar, builders usually use a mortar that is weaker than the stone, so that if cracks do form, they run down the mortar lines and not through the stone. As long as cracking stays within the mortar, a wall can be repaired through repointing (replacing the mortar) and the stones themselves won't require replacement. Stone is laid either in horizontal courses, or in a random pattern. If the stones are irregular in shape, we have a rubble pattern. If they are cut into rectilinear blocks, the pattern is called ashlar.

Stone, because of its longevity, has been used through millennia for the most "important" buildings: the ones societies wanted to last. There exist today stone buildings that are over 4,000 years old. Some quarries also have very long lives. There are travertine quarries near Rome that were around during the heyday of the Roman Empire, and the Carrara marble quarry, started by Caesar Augustus and favored by Michelangelo, is still in use today.

But, as brick became cheaper, the use of stone dwindled. Stone was used on the outer, publicly visible layer of the building, while brick (or in many cases, rough types of concrete) was used on the interior. A common building practice was to set the outer stone and use it as formwork for the brick or concrete inner walls.

Structural stone buildings are considered valuable today, and their durability allows them to undergo a number of "lifetimes," often with different uses. But because of the cost of their material and difficulty of construction, almost all stone buildings today are merely veneer (sometimes only ⅛-inch thick) attached to a concrete frame.

WHAT IS THE DIFFERENCE BETWEEN CONCRETE AND CEMENT?

When you were a kid riding your bike down the sidewalk, your parents most likely said, "Don't fall down and skin your knees on the cement." Well, more technically, they should have warned you about the concrete.

Cement is a fine powder, which is now made most commonly by mixing lime, iron, silica, and alumina, heating it to around 2,600 to 3,000 degrees Fahrenheit, and mixing it with gypsum. The pulverized end product is called portland cement, and is only one ingredient of concrete.

To make concrete, you mix gravel and sand with cement and water. The water starts a chemical reaction in the cement (which gives off heat in the

The Romans invented concrete in the second century A.D. They mixed lime mortar with pozzalana stone, which forms a strong, slow-curing cement.

process) that causes the cement to harden and bind together the gravel and sand. The gravel and sand are there because they add strength to the hardened cement as well as resistance to shrinkage and cracking.

Besides the basic elements, there are many other ingredients one might find in concrete. Additives (called admixtures) give concrete added chemical resistance, strength, hardness, stiffness or flexibility, and even color (though coloring concrete often doesn't work as well as one might think it should).

The Romans first developed concrete in the second century A.D. At that time, they were used to building with bricks held together with lime mortar. But things changed when they found a mineral from Mount Vesuvius they called pozzolana, which could be mixed with the lime mortar to form a strong, slow-curing cement. They quickly learned that gravel and sand mixed with the pozzolana and lime created a universal construction material that hardened even under water. Its plastic properties meant that the final shape of whatever they were building depended mostly on the skill of those building the forms.

The Romans carted their pozzolana all across their empire to mix with local lime, gravel, and sand and create concrete buildings, aqueducts, walls, and subwater piers. Some of these works can still be seen, more than three-quarters of a millennia later, in ruins all across Europe.

The Dark Ages that followed the fall of the Roman Empire put an end to concrete for almost fifteen centuries. The miracle of cement, sand, gravel, and water was rediscovered in the nineteenth century, and has again made its mark on architecture. This time, though, we've discovered the further miracle of steel reinforcement, which allows shapes, spans, and heights the Romans could never hope to achieve.

What is Steel-Reinforced Concrete?

Concrete is very strong in compression (you can put a lot of weight on top of it). It is not very strong in tension (you can't hang too much weight from it), shear (sliding/tearing force), or moment resistance (it can snap in two). Steel, which is about as strong in tension as compression, and offers significant shear and moment resistance, is the material of choice for reinforcing concrete elements that must resist more than compression. For example, floor slabs cannot sag and crack in the middle, so they need moment resistance. Their weight cannot make them break off where they connect to the columns, so they need shear resistance. And, many times, heavy things like lights or ceilings have to hang from them, so they need tensile strength.

Reinforced concrete was a new and exciting material in the 1920s and 1930s, and was a major contributing factor to the development in Europe of what became modern architecture (it was first developed at the turn of the twentieth century in the United States as a building material for grain silos and low-rise factories). In the United States, Frank Lloyd Wright, particularly, is known for his work with reinforced concrete.

Concrete is an economical material for holding up buildings, and it can be made quite attractive without additional finishing. Its fluidity during placement, and monolithic solidness and strength once it's set, means a number of forms and structural amusements and amazements are possible. One is the cantilever. If a building material is stiff enough and has enough weight on one end, it can extend out, seemingly unsupported, an impressive distance (sort of like a gangplank).

There is a story that Wright designed such a cantilever out of reinforced concrete. Construction workers dutifully built the forms, placed the reinforcement, and poured the concrete, but were concerned that once the forms were removed, the concrete would break and fall. Wright, according to the story, was so confident of his design that he stood under the concrete slab and kicked out the timbers holding up the form.

Another designer who experimented with reinforced concrete in the days before World War II was an Italian structural engineer named Pier Luigi Nervi. He developed what is called *ferrocement*, in which layers of concrete and steel mesh create an inexpensive but extremely durable building material. Nervi designed ferrocement airplane hangars in Italy that were so strong that they structurally survived the German army's attempts to dynamite them during World War II. Ferrocement isn't as common on the construction site as steel-bar-reinforced concrete because it is so difficult to put the wire mesh and concrete in place in a hurry.

During the 1950s and 1960s, a technique called *post-tensioning* was developed that took advantage of concrete's compressive strength and the ability of steel to maintain compressive stress when stretched and held

Pier Luigi Nervi's Pallazzetto dello Sport in Rome uses a precast concrete shell roof covering a 200-foot-wide space.

14

(just as a rubber band holds things together). To post-tension concrete, workers place tubes in the formwork that stretch from one end to the other of the concrete piece to be poured. The tubes keep the concrete from sticking to steel rods (called *tendons*) inside.

Once the concrete is set, powerful jacks attached to the ends of the tendons stretch the steel ever so slightly but store a tremendous amount of force. Grout (similar to concrete but with smaller gravel) is pumped in around the tendon, which, once it cures, keeps the tendon stretched in place. The result of storing all this force is that concrete pieces can be made thinner and more lightweight but still work as hard. Commonly used in beams and floor slabs of tall concrete-frame buildings, post-tensioning allows thinner structural elements and floors, which means more interior space.

In more recent engineering developments, there is a concept that takes the combination of these two materials beyond the stage where the steel serves only to reinforce concrete. In composite systems, steel and concrete reinforce each other. Concrete—typically of the high-strength variety—when placed in hollow steel columns combines the strengths of the two materials so that thinner, lighter columns are possible (which means not only more space inside, but also that buildings can be built taller).

Another symbiotic combination of the two materials has been to bury the ends of structural steel columns and beams in a large slab of concrete, which holds the steel firmly in place without too much fuss over how accurately the steel elements are welded or bolted together.

Although the relationship of steel and concrete has some problems (for one thing, they shrink and expand differently; for another thing, steel rusts when it falls in with bad company such as water and the minerals that often hang out with water), it looks like these two materials will be together for a long, long time.

SHOULD I WORRY ABOUT CRACKS IN A CONCRETE BUILDING?

On the one hand, no. On the other hand, especially if they're stained, yes. It all depends on where the cracks are and how they are forming.

An unavoidable characteristic of concrete is that it cracks. Especially as it dries during curing, microscopic cracks always form in concrete—mostly the result of a tremendous number of minute stress lines as the concrete shrinks. There are ways to control such cracking. Reinforcement, fibers, meshes, and rods, mostly of steel or glass, minimize concrete shrinkage and subsequent cracking.

Regardless of how much antishrink reinforcement is put into curing concrete, though, it still shrinks and it still cracks. What this means is that individual concrete pieces—floor slabs, columns, beams, and so on—simply can't be so large that the combined force of all the microscopic cracking gang up and make big cracks. You'll notice, if you look at a sidewalk or patio, for instance, that there are grooves in large expanses of concrete, or complete separations filled with tar or oakum. Usually those cracks (the ones that will break your mother's back, according to that somewhat violent nursery rhyme) divide the stretch of concrete into squares. Those are cracking control joints.

Where the concrete does not have to be structurally continuous or monolithic, control joints separate adjoining pieces of a slab or wall completely. If, as is usually the case, the control joint has to be waterproof, it is caulked or otherwise sealed against moisture penetration in a way that allows heat- and cold-induced expansion and contraction. Allowing the concrete sections to move independently reduces cracking. When the wall or slab has to be one structural piece, a strategy is to form or cut grooves into the concrete to concentrate the cracking in a controlled way.

Cracking is bad in reinforced concrete, not so much because it weakens the concrete but because it lets in water that rusts the reinforcing steel. If the designers predetermine where cracks will occur, they can also plan precautions against corrosion of reinforcement beneath crack control joints.

Structurally speaking, cracking is a somewhat desirable property for this particular material. Unlike metal, concrete doesn't bend much before it breaks. Hooke's Law states that in its *elastic state*, strain in a material (its ability to resist force) equals the stress (exterior force) put on it until the material reaches its *plastic state*. At that point a material deforms (bends, twists, or buckles) until it fails and breaks. Steel beams and columns are flexible relative to concrete, and resist a lot of force when they flex or sway (in the elastic state, energy is dissipated mostly as heat). Steel also absorbs a lot of energy when it deforms (plastic state). When steel

A close-up view of Nervi's Little Palace of Sports shows how well-mixed, well-poured, and well-connected concrete can keep cracking to a minimum.

17

cracks, it is at the end of its road toward failure, so any cracking in steel is cause for serious concern.

Concrete isn't very flexible at all, so it can't resist force by flexing and swaying. Moreover, it tends to fail without spending much time in the plastic state. Instead of dissipating energy in the form of heat and deformation, concrete dissipates energy through cracking. In its elastic state, concrete cracks ever so minutely, and cracks aren't connected. As stress loads build, cracks enlarge, connect, and then enlarge some more up until the concrete breaks. So concrete cracks when it is working hard to resist force. Such cracking, for the most part, is invisible to the unaided eye.

Cracking is a bad sign when it indicates that the concrete is of poor quality or that something is going wrong beneath the surface, especially corrosion of iron or steel reinforcement or attachment pieces.

Concrete works very well when used for the right purpose and in the right way. Serious flaws are the result either of improper design, improper workmanship, or a combination of both. Design flaws mostly involve lack of protection against penetration by water and salts or failure on the part of the designer to recognize the properties of concrete or the vagaries of construction techniques. It often is an imperfect world at the construction site and mistakes in mixing, forming, curing, and finishing can create a lot of cracks that may or may not be serious to the building structure.

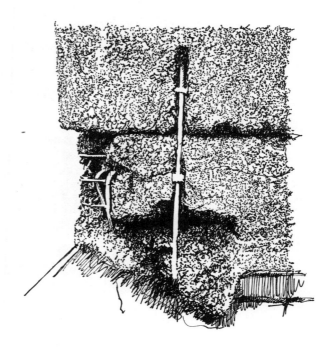

Cracks in concrete are most serious when they allow water and corrosive salts to penetrate to reinforcing steel.

There are many kinds of concrete, each made with its own specific ingredient list and mixing instructions. There also are many ways to reinforce concrete. If the concrete isn't strong enough for the job, is too water absorbent, doesn't resist chemicals in the atmosphere at the building site, or in any way isn't up to the forces and degradations it must face, the concrete will deteriorate, crack, and ultimately fail. Good design is anticipating and designing around such problems.

Water is always a problem and often the chief culprit in concrete cracking. If it penetrates into concrete and freezes, the ice expands with enough force to make cracks. Each time this happens (a freeze-thaw cycle), the cracks get bigger, the force of expanding water stronger, and the concrete weaker. Water also attacks metal, especially water that contains salts from masonry or the ground. Corroding metal expands and weakens when it corrodes, which means cracking concrete and decreased reinforcement strength. (Corrosion cracks are recognizable from the regular patterns they form and from the rust-colored stains that often occur along the crack lines.)

Construction problems start with the mixing of water, sand, cement, aggregate, and admixtures. Too little water, for instance, may provide insufficient cure and the concrete won't be as solid and strong as it needs to be. Too much water can also cause surface damage (because the thin concrete leaks from the forms or cures improperly) which is both unsightly and an invitation to water penetration or similar deterioration. Sometimes careless workers leave trash or other debris in the forms, which can cause pieces of concrete to pop out much later.

With large concrete projects, formwork has to be removed quickly enough that the subsequent pour blends aesthetically and structurally with the one before. On the other hand, formwork can't be removed too quickly, or surface damage can occur. And, once the formwork is off, the concrete must be allowed to cure for a period of a few hours to several weeks—depending on the specifics of the job—before it develops enough strength to do its intended job.

WHAT IS THE DIFFERENCE BETWEEN IRON AND STEEL?

Pure iron is an element (the fourth most common element in the world) and steel is an iron alloy, one might say. But it's not as simple as that. Iron doesn't occur in its pure state in nature, and people were deriving metal from iron long before they understood its elemental makeup. So, over time, names have been given to ferrous metals based on their physical properties—a function of molecular structure—not whether the metals are pure or alloyed iron.

Wrought iron and cast iron were two early ferrous metals. The former can be heated and hammered into shape, while brittle cast iron has to be molded. Carbon steel with a tough surface (which holds an edge well for

Steel is an iron alloy and it (not iron) is the metal used for structural members.

tools and weapons) was produced in small quantities soon after. And, with the relatively recent development of the Bessemer process, large quantities of mild steel—which is strong in compression and tension and can be rolled into uniform sections—became affordable for holding up buildings. All four of these metals contain iron and carbon. Wrought iron is the purest, followed by mild steel, cast iron, and carbon steel.

Metallurgy has advanced, mostly over the past two centuries, to a point where special mixing with carbon, chromium, nickel, and other elements, and various combinations of hot and cold forming treatments, produce a whole range of steels that have attributes specifically suited in terms of strength and corrosion resistance to many specialized tasks.

Early technology was limited by the heat that could be generated for smeltering. Because bellows-driven smithy furnaces couldn't generate enough heat to melt pure iron (2,797 degrees Fahrenheit is needed for that), early smiths developed two iron-making processes. When iron ore is heated to a spongy mass in an oxidizing fire and stirred (a process called *puddling*) the result is wrought iron, which is heavy, hard, strong, and easier to work than bronze (the preferred metal before 1000 B.C., when the Iron Age began).

Alternatively, iron mixed with carbides lowers the melting temperature to within the capabilities of early furnaces. Cast iron is the result. It is easier to mold complex shapes with cast iron than it is to forge them with wrought iron. But cast iron is brittle and, although strong in compression, doesn't have the tensile strength of wrought iron.

Steel was first developed from wrought iron. Blacksmiths found that if they wrought a piece of white hot iron and left it on the coals for some time, the resulting metal was tougher than the original piece of iron. It was time consuming to make the resulting metal, and ironsmiths didn't really understand how it all worked (a slow transfer of carbon from the charcoal fire to the surface of the iron). But the carbon steel made better weapons and tools, so it was all worthwhile for the time being.

Because of its relative abundance and lower cost, iron found its way into buildings much earlier than steel. Processes for mass producing wrought iron and cast iron were developed in the eighteenth century, and ironworking changed from a craft into an industry. Once it was plentiful, the fire-resistant properties and strength of iron made it a natural for the first large-frame buildings. (William Strutt used cast iron beams for a factory floor structure in Britain, and in 1885 William Jenney used an all-iron structural frame that supported a curtain-wall enclosure.)

Developments in steel production in the nineteenth century introduced steel to construction, which allowed engineers to create structural shapes and heights that had never before been possible. Henry Bessemer invented a process in 1856 that made steel plentiful for the first time. The Bessemer converter blows superheated air through molten pig iron (unrefined cast iron), which burns off much of the carbon, as well as impurities such as silicon, sulfur, phosphorus, and manganese. The resulting mild steel is cheaper to make than wrought iron. (As a result, nearly all of what is sold as wrought iron these days for fences, lamps, and other decorative items is actually low-carbon rolled steel.)

Throughout the twentieth century, the cost of labor has risen much more sharply than the cost of materials. Because steel construction is less labor intensive than masonry to produce the same-size building, steel became popular in building construction even though it is more expensive than brick or concrete. To be fair, concrete construction frequently proves more economical than steel in many localities because of differing availabilities of skilled labor and material. But remember that it was the introduction of steel reinforcement that made concrete the popular building material it has become.

As steel has become a smash hit on the construction market, a new aesthetic has arisen. Building owners once bought cast-iron facades for their building fronts (around the turn of the last century) as a cheaper way to get the solid, well-built look of stone. Now, with the original intent long forgotten, cast-iron facades have an aesthetic appeal all their own, and fiberglass replicas of cast iron are popping up to mock the mocker.

In a similar vein, a current trend is to create whatever basic configuration a designer might want by building a steel-frame skeleton, then creating the desired outward appearance with a thin layer of stone, sheet metal, concrete, or even stucco applied directly to reinforced insulation board. Space frames, with their minimal use of material and maximal flexibility of shape, push the range of possible building shapes even further (see pp. 75–76). In a large part, steel makes that possible. And, of course, iron makes steel possible.

WHO FIRST USED STRUCTURAL STEEL IN BUILDINGS?

William Le Baron Jenney (1832–1907) was a Chicago architect born in Fair Haven, Massachusetts. With a family in the whaling business, Jenney spent time at sea early in his life, and was impressed by the structural elegance of the bamboo-framed houses he saw in the Philippines, a concept he would later transfer to iron. Interested in engineering, he attended Harvard before going to Paris to the Ecole Centrale des Arts et Manufactures, from which he graduated with honors in 1856. While in

The Home Insurance Building in Chicago is the first example of the use of structural steel for spandrel girders. Designed by William Le Baron Jenney, it was constructed in 1885.

Paris, Jenney was influenced by teachers who stressed the compatibility through design of materials, function, and structure. He also knew of a warehouse built on the Paris docks, completed in 1866, which was the first multistory, fireproofed building with concrete floors and curtain walls. Those were elements of the work Jenney was to produce shortly thereafter.

Jenney served as an officer under Grant and Sherman during the Civil War, moved to Chicago in 1867, and opened his own architecture office in 1868. Jenney practiced in Chicago until 1905, when he moved to Los Angeles, two years before his death.

Jenney made his biggest mark in history between 1884 and 1885 when the Home Insurance Building was built. Jenney's design, in association with engineer George B. Whitney, called for nine stories, the top three stories of which were built with steel girders. (Another two stories were added in 1891.)

The columns in this building, the first one to contain structural steel, were made of cast and wrought iron. Up to the sixth floor, girders and floor beams were wrought iron. It was the spandrel girders framing the upper two floors that introduced steel to high-rise frame construction.

There was never really a *first* skyscraper, since a number of architects were designing iron-framed, laterally reinforced buildings in Chicago and New York simultaneously during the 1880s. And it is argued that the Home Insurance Building is not a skyscraper, since masonry in the foundation and walls also carries the building's weight, and the frame did not include lateral bracing (necessary in skyscrapers to resist the force of the wind). But for those who want to single out one building as a landmark achievement in the development of the modern steel-framed skyscraper, the Home Insurance Building and its designer, William Le Baron Jenney, serve nicely.

WHAT IS THE DIFFERENCE BETWEEN LUMBER AND TIMBER? HARDWOOD AND SOFTWOOD?

In general terms, wood prepared and used for construction work is called timber in Great Britain and lumber in the United States. Strictly speaking, any wood called *timber* in America is still in the ground and growing. However, just to cloud the issue, sawed pieces of lumber with a 4- by 6-inch or greater cross section are called timbers, especially by builders. (Don't worry if you're confused. So is everybody.)

These large wood building components are called timbers (as in "heavy timber construction") even though technically they are lumber.

Hardwood and softwood are *botanical* classifications, and have nothing to do with the strength of the materials. For instance, balsa, the material of choice for model airplanes, is technically a hardwood. Hardwoods come from deciduous trees, such as oak and maple, which lose their broad-shaped leaves in the fall. Hardwood is most commonly used for flooring, and for the smaller pieces of construction, such as moldings, trims, and stair treads.

Softwoods come from coniferous, or evergreen trees, including the many varieties of pine and fir. Softwood is used for most wood construction in the United States: for posts and beams, roofs, and foundations. Wood siding, shingles, and shakes almost always are made of softwood. Redwood and cedar are two varieties of softwood that have natural decay resistance, which makes them suitable for outdoor use without paint or finishes (although they do wear away some from sunlight and rain, which is what gives them that gray, rough, "weathered" look).

As our forest supplies diminish, and pieces of lumber large enough for construction grow scarcer and more expensive, we have sought cheaper alternatives to solid wood in building. One example is ubiquitous plywood, in which several (usually three to seven) thin sheets ("plies") are glued together to form a large sheet of wood. To make a beam or an arch, the same principle is used: gluing together thin layers formed in the appropriate shape. The result is called *glued, laminated* lumber, or *glulam* for short. Although glulams are cheaper than solid wood, they are as strong or stronger. The glue that holds the wood plies together is stronger than the wood itself.

Other types of "manufactured" wood abound in board form. They include particle boards, which are a mix of small flakes or chips of hard- or softwood into an adhesive binder, somewhat like walnuts baked into brownies. Fiberboards follow the same recipe, substituting strands of wood fiber for the flakes. You may hear them called *strandboards* or *spaghetti boards*.

Why don't two-by-fours measure 2 by 4 inches?

First of all, a two-by-four connotes the cross-section measurements of a piece of lumber; that piece can be any length. But a two-by-four today actually measures 1½ inches by 3½ inches. The name of the piece of lumber is still "two-by-four," the *nominal* size; 1½ inches by 3½ inches is the *actual* size.

Sizing of lumber resembles the "quarter pounder" syndrome at hamburger joints: By law, the quarter pounder you purchase weighs a quarter of a pound before it is cooked. By the time the burger's grease is fried out and its moisture evaporated by cooking, it weighs less than a quarter of a pound.

In residential construction two-by-fours usually comprise the major structural components.

In a similar manner, at the time the two-by-four was sawn, it was probably close to measuring 2 inches by 4 inches. To remove moisture and stiffen up this "green" piece of wood, it is kiln dried, a process known as *seasoning*. This causes the two-by-four to shrink to about 5 percent of its original size (which, admittedly, is a small portion of its size).

The seasoned two-by-four loses the lion's share of its original dimension through a process known as *dressing*. Most lumber sold today is dressed, which means it is sanded smooth with a planing machine on any or all four faces, depending on its intended use. The two-system measure (nominal or actual) for lumber harks back to an earlier time, when it was common for mills to sell lumber in rough-sawn form. The even dimensions were those of the rough-sawn lumber, while the fractions were for the fancier product: dressed lumber.

Building with wood requires more "forgiveness" within the structural system than building with steel or concrete. Forgiveness means that the pieces of wood can vary, within acceptable limits, in strength, size, and straightness, yet the structure can still be built to hold up the building. Wood, after all, is an organic product. Even after seasoning, it contains a changeable moisture content within its cell structure, which causes it to shrink and swell. (The reason your wood front door "sticks" when it rains is because it has "grown" in size from the moisture in its cells.) In addition, different manufacturers use different tolerances. Builders learn to deal with this; constructing a wood-frame building is not as precise as making a Swiss watch, or even constructing a steel building, where the manufacturing process can be and is controlled much more carefully. But quality wood construction does involve a high level of craftsmanship. For one thing, wood joints must allow for movement from changing moisture but still be tight so the building doesn't wobble.

The dimensions of dimensional wood have changed over the years. Most have gotten smaller. A 150-year-old building may have been built with two-by-fours that were actually 2 inches by 4 inches, while a 50-year-old building may have been built with members that were actually 1¾ inches by 3¾ inches. One clue to determining the actual size of the wood from drawings is that standard notation requires that the nominal measurements be written without inch marks ("), while actual dimensions are given inch marks. The rule of thumb is that if you want to know the size of a piece of wood, forget about reading labels. Get out and measure it.

Why are there no wooden skyscrapers?

Probably the biggest reason is fire. Great fires in Chicago, San Francisco, Baltimore, New York, and other urban centers in the 1890s through 1910s convinced city dwellers that they needed building codes to protect themselves from the threat of fire to so many buildings so close together (see pp. 103–104). Wood as a material is very difficult to fireproof, so strict limits were put on its use in buildings, including the size a wooden structure could be.

Other reasons have to do with wood's general unsuitability for the stresses a building must strain to contain. For one thing, tall buildings rely on fairly strict limits as to how much a building can vary from being

Fear of fire limits the height of most wood buildings. This eighteenth-century Russian Church on the island of Khizi is one of the world's tallest wood buildings.

straight up and down. Dimensional movement from temperature and humidity makes wood structures go rickety over time if they're too tall in relation to the width and depth of the building. Uneven floors are another outcome of the dimensional instability of wood. The joints that are possible with wood add further limitations of strength and flexibility over time, although steel-bracket joinery and automated, high-precision tooling do allow considerable design flexibility. Very tall wood structures are possible, but they have to be so broad at the base, have so much cross bracing, and are such a fire risk that the end result just wouldn't compete well with concrete or steel.

Wood is a strong material, yet it can be shaped and joined with hand tools. It can withstand being pulled or pushed with a lot of compressive or tensile force. It is stiff enough to resist day-to-day forces, yet flexible enough to withstand the sudden rocking and jolts of storms or earthquakes. And wood can be treated and shaped into all sorts of configurations. But heavy lumbering throughout the United States and Canada over the past few centuries has made large-dimension lumber pretty much a thing of the past, and now we see most large wooden structural elements made out of many smaller pieces of wood laminated or otherwise attached together.

Technical know-how in glues have made laminated wood a reliable, attractive, and competitively priced structural material. It still isn't fireproof, but as pieces of wood get smaller and the percentage of binder in laminated wood goes up, many of the other properties of wood do change. For one thing, dimensional stability increases. For another thing, which may or may not be significant to the reader, the smells we associate with wood decrease.

The fact of the matter is that wood and plastic binders are steadily making inroads into the construction industry. And the day may come—when the fireproofing and dimensional stability issues are chemically thwarted—that high-rise structures will be wooden. Or at least they may contain a lot of wood.

WHY DO TALL COMMERCIAL BUILDINGS USE SHINY GLASS?

There is a style of thinking in architecture that says that building form should expose its structure; like a bridge, the elements that hold it up are what make it beautiful. Such is the original thinking behind what are now called glass boxes, but once were more popularly called the international style (from the International Exposition in Paris where such architects as Mies van der Rohe, Walter Gropius, and Corbusier created the interest

Skidmore, Owings & Merrill's Lever House in New York set a standard for glass tower design when it was built in 1952.

that later became a style). The building many consider the original glass tower is the Lever House in New York City, designed by Skidmore, Owings & Merrill in 1952. Arguably, large glass boxes that reflect the sky and the buildings around it make less of a visual impact than large concrete- or stone-clad buildings.

In the 1970s, though, energy became a major concern, and glass on buildings took a public-relations beating. In the south, glass allowed too much heat in from the sun's radiant heat and made air-conditioning costs skyrocket. In the north, glass, which is a poor insulator, let too much heat out by way of convection. For a very short while, it looked as if glass boxes were on the way out.

A few changes in manufacturing and design revived the popularity of glass. For large commercial buildings, reflective coatings allowed light in, but not radiant heat. Some were bronze or blue, others have been developed that look no different from nontreated glass. Furthermore, awnings and building overhangs were rediscovered to control the amount of sunlight allowed to enter through windows.

To keep heat within buildings, insulated windows—double- or triple-glazed, some with insulating gas filling between panes of glass—and careful orientation of windows to gain solar heat during colder months—made glass more energy efficient than insulated sheathings.

With the energy problems smoothed out to a large extent, and with the glass manufacturers as aggressive as ever in marketing their glazing products, it looks as if glass-covered towers are here to stay, at least for a little while longer.

Why don't we have plastic buildings (yet)?

We don't have plastic "buildings" because buildings typically are classified by their structural frames. Although there are plastics available that are *strong* enough to serve as framing for some kinds of buildings, there is no structural plastic available yet that can stand heat over 400 degrees Fahrenheit. Since building fires can easily reach temperatures of over 2,000 degrees Fahrenheit, and because many plastics release toxic fumes when they burn, plastics clearly do not fit the structural bill.

Plastics *in* buildings, however, are another story. There are now over 10,000 kinds of plastics in the world, and many find their way into almost any nonstructural building component you can think of: sheet and tile flooring, gutters, downspouts, moldings, clapboards, siding, window frames, pipes, drainage systems, facings for sandwich panels, insulating foams, paints, adhesives, binders, vapor barriers, and wiring. They can be divided basically into two types: *thermoset* (permanently hard once they're cured) and *thermoplastic* (soften over and over again when heated and harden when cooled).

The first plastic, vinyl, was concocted in 1828 by French chemists. It was used mostly as a molded replacement for natural materials like ivory and tortoiseshell in small novelty items, such as combs. Plastics did not enter the building industry until just after the turn of the century, when they made their debut mostly as small parts, such as electrical sockets. In 1925, polystyrene (now used in foam insulation) became commercially available, heralding an enthusiasm for the material in a big way. *Popular Science* magazine in the 1930s said, "the American of Tomorrow . . .

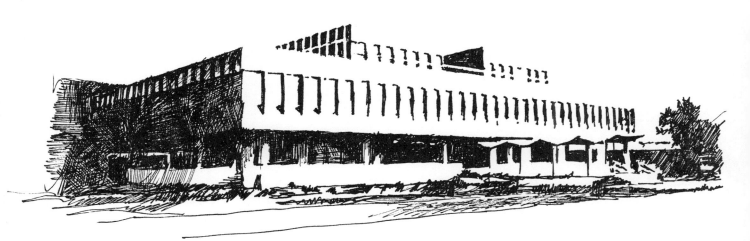

One application of plastic in buildings is to replace ornate stonework. Although fiber-reinforced plastic looks like stone and withstands weathering, it is not suitable for structural use.

clothed in plastics from head to foot . . . will live in a plastics house, drive a plastics automobile, and fly in a plastics airplane."

Over a half a century later, we have not lived up to that prophecy, but we are getting closer. According to General Electric's plastics division, the building and construction industry is currently the largest market in the world for plastics (packaging is second, and car bodies are third). Plastics still have a reputation to live down, though: They have always been cheap substitutes for other materials (vinyl for wood siding, pvc for steel pipe). In the vernacular, a phony person is called "plastic"; a President impervious to criticism is deemed "Teflon." One could say that plastics—because their properties and shapes are carefully devised and predictable—have no architectural genre of their own.

Image aside, the other major stumbling block to widespread use of plastic is its parentage. It is made from petroleum, a nonrenewable resource. And thermoplastics do not rust, corrode, or degrade—ideal properties for building materials, terrible traits for waste materials. As the plastics industries explore new methods for plastics recycling, its chances of being an environmentally acceptable building material are improving dramatically.

WHY DO THEY PUT TAR ON ROOFS?

Anyone who has watched builders deal with the heat and the smell of tarring a roof (especially at noon on a summer's day) has probably wondered why they have to do it. The reason is simple: This technique, called *built-up roofing,* is a tried and true method of waterproofing a flat roof.

Asphalt, the waterproof "tar" used on flat roofs, forms a black roofscape of the city.

The "tar" is actually asphalt, composed of solid or semisolid hydrocarbons obtained from the distillation of petroleum or coal. It is liquified by heating, then mopped on the flat roof surface. When it cools, the asphalt forms a one-piece, waterproof membrane. (The flat roof, by the way, most likely has some pitch to it—roofs that are dead level or perfectly flat are sitting ducks for ponds of water.)

It takes some skill and effort, and a fair amount of time, to construct a well-made built-up roof. The roofer assembles a built-up roof membrane in place from multiple layers (*plies*) of asphalt-impregnated felt made of cellulose fibers or glass fibers. While the asphalt does the waterproofing, the felts serve as reinforcement for the asphalt, giving it a more solid form. The felt is saturated with asphalt at the factory and delivered to the site in rolls, which the builder lays down on the roof surface over a layer of asphalt. The rolls of felt are laid down in overlapping layers, so that there are no seams that might allow the water to seep down to the roof structure. Another layer of hot asphalt is mopped on; it softens the asphalt in the felt so that the whole gooey mess sticks together. Normally, an odd number of felt plies goes into construction of a built-up roof. Three or five plies is typical. A rule of thumb: The more plies used, the more durable the roof and the longer it can be expected to last. Once the plies have been mopped on, the layered concoction is covered with a *flood coat* of asphalt. Sometimes, if the pitch of the roof is not too steep, a layer of small stones, called *aggregate,* is embedded in the surface. The aggregate allows a heavier flood coat of asphalt to stick, which means better moisture protection and better protection from degradation caused by ultraviolet light. Aggregate also helps keep the roof membrane from getting too hot.

Derivatives of built-up roofing include asphalt shingles, made of heavy felt impregnated and coated with asphalt; and sheets of asphalt, which are about ¾-inch thick and applied directly to the roof deck.

Although built-up roofing is a tried and true application for relatively flat roofs, it is getting a run for its money from a roofing method developed in the 1970s, called single-ply roofing. As its name implies, this method entails placing a single layer of roofing, usually a plastic or rubber, down on the roof deck. Its clean and easy application accounts for its rapidly growing popularity. According to the National Roofing Association, in 1988 about 37 percent of roofing in the commercial market (where roofs tend to be flat) were built-up roofs; 29 percent were single-plies, and the rest were other types, including metal roofs. In the typically pitched-roof residential market, 67 percent of the roofs were shingle, and only 4 percent were built up. Built-up roofs are more popular in the West and South, while single-plies are catching on most quickly in the Northeast and Midwest.

Why do copper roofs turn green?

The unique bluish-green of aged copper results when the metal's surface oxidizes upon exposure to the atmosphere, in much the same way that rust forms on iron. Called the *patina*, this bluish-green coating is actually good for the copper, because, unlike rust, patina forms a tight shield that prevents further corrosion of the copper underneath. The greenish blue color itself comes from the formation of copper sulfates.

The corrosion process of copper continues naturally for about seventy-five years, and then stops. The natural reddish-gold of the copper first turns silver, then gray, then (after about ten years) begins to take on the characteristic bluish-green. After about twenty-five years, the color of the patina will not change. If the patina is scraped off, the copper below will appear as its natural reddish-gold, and the corrosion and color cycle will begin again.

If architects wish to preserve the original copper color, they can specify that the copper roof be coated with clear acrylic. Oxygen and water therefore will not come in contact with the copper itself, and the corrosion process cannot take place.

Washington State's Tacoma Union Station (completed in 1913) has a copper roof.

Copper is ubiquitous in building use, partly because it is found in all parts of the world, and also because it is hard, strong, and malleable (it can be beaten into shapes without cracking). Archeologists have found copper artifacts dating back to 8500 B.C. One of the earliest architectural uses dates to 7000 B.C., when huge copper doors graced Egyptian temples.

During the Gothic period, copper roofs were used extensively. The oldest known example is the Cathedral of Hildesheim in Germany, which was competed in 1230 A.D. When, tragically, it was destroyed during World War II, its original copper roof was still intact. The great cathedrals at Chartres, Canterbury, and the Notre Dame de Paris all have copper roofs.

The other reason for copper's widespread use is its excellence as a conductor of heat and electricity. In fact, most of the copper used in buildings today takes the form of wiring and piping. A good portion of today's copper also goes into the production of architectural brass (copper combined with zinc) and bronze (copper combined with tin).

WHAT IS PAINT MADE OF?

Paint in all its many forms and types can be broken down into three basic components: pigments for color, a binder (called the *vehicle*), and a solvent. A particular kind of paint also may contain any number of additives to give it special properties, from fire resistance to bacteria and fungus resistance.

The major breakthroughs in paints throughout the ages have been developments of the binders, which have made paints increasingly useful for a number of purposes. Although paints in buildings today are used as much for protection from the elements as they are for aesthetic reasons, the earliest paints were solely for decorative purposes. Egyptian tombs dating from 2600 B.C. sport large painted areas that are still visible today. Craftsmen of that era mixed pigments with binders of tree gum, raw eggs, or milk proteins so that the colors would not rub off the wall. Such paints made with water-soluble vehicles today are called *distemper* or *tempera paints*.

Another major breakthrough in increasing the permanency of coloring is fresco painting, developed by the Minoan civilization, which thrived on Crete between 3000 B.C. and 1100 B.C. In this technique craftsmen first cover the wall to be painted with lime plaster, and then paint directly on the wet plaster with pigments mixed with lime water. The carbon dioxide in the air reacts with the lime to form calcium carbonate, and the colors become insoluble in water. Fresco painting remained a popular technique throughout the seventeenth century.

By the eighteenth century, water and water-soluble glues as binders were rivaled in popularity by oil-based paints, normally made with linseed oil. The next major development in paint binders occurred in the 1930s, when synthetic polymers were first used as paint vehicles, both as an alternative to oil and in conjunction with oil. These paints are classified as enamels—very-high-gloss, high-gloss, semigloss, and flat. The difference between the various degrees of gloss is due to the pigment-vehicle concentration. The vehicle in any of these paints can be oil, a mixture of oil and synthetic resin, or synthetic resin.

In 1949, water-based paints using synthetic polymers were introduced. They are called plastic paints, latex paints, or emulsion paints. They have become very popular because they can be thinned with water, and brushes and rollers can be cleaned with soap and warm water.

While binders have developed steadily over the centuries, the use of pigments has remained comparatively constant. Although some pigments are manufactured synthetically, many derive from the same sources as they did millennia ago. For instance, the white marble of the Parthenon was originally brightly painted, with yellow ochre and sienna and umber from the earth, ultramarine blue from lapis lazuli (a semiprecious stone), and red from iron oxide.

San Francisco's colorful Victorian row houses are painted so freely and cheerfully that they are referred to as "painted ladies."

40

Despite its use since ancient times, paint applied incorrectly can develop a number of common problems. Knowing the causes can suggest probable cures and help prevent them in the future. Some of the problems that can occur with paint and their probable causes include the following.

Alligatoring, a severe form of cracking, results when a surface is covered with several coats of paint, which over time have lost the ability to expand and contract at the same rate as the painted surface.

Blistering occurs when water sitting on the paint's surface dissolves the paint's soluble ingredient. A bubble forms under the top layer of paint and draws more and more water until the bubble breaks under pressure and blisters the surface (just like a blister on your big toe). Blistering is most likely to happen if one of the paint ingredients, say the pigment, contains water-soluble salts.

Flaking happens when moisture enters at a joint, such as where the wall meets the ground or the roof, and gets under the paint film. The moisture causes lack of adhesion of the paint film to the building surface, and the paint flakes off.

Peeling, like flaking, occurs when moisture gets behind the paint film surface (again, usually at the joints). Peeling usually occurs in hot weather, when the trapped water vaporizes and tries to force its way out, breaking up the paint film in the process.

Mildew is caused by fungus deposited from the air onto the paint surface. It can be prevented by special paint containing mildewcide.

Wrinkling can result if too thick a coat of paint was applied to the building surface. Or, if the paint is overmixed, a portion of it may have too much drying agent. That portion may wrinkle after the paint dries.

CAN I PULL OUT THAT SOFT GRAY YUCK BETWEEN BUILDING PANELS?

No! (Maybe you *can*, but you shouldn't.) The soft gray (or white or black) stuff in between the panels is sealant, and although it may look useless, it is likely there for a number of reasons. The sealant may have been installed to improve the building's appearance, but foremost, a sealant prevents water from entering the building at its joints or seams, where building components come together. Second, it stops air infiltration into and out of the building. Third, it allows movement and settling of the individual building components, somewhat like a car's shock absorbers.

Many sealants look removable because they are gunned into place while wet, and shrink as they cure or dry. Sometimes a piece of the resulting rubberlike mass protrudes from its joint in the building, looking extraneous. (Sealants that you can pull out are not the structural kind. If installed correctly, structural sealants cling tightly to the sides of the building, and because of their chemical composition, do not shrink as they cure. They are made to last about twenty years.)

Sealants are very temperature sensitive, and the time of year that they are applied can make a big difference as to whether they protrude from the joints. A sealant applied in the summer may have to overstretch in the winter as the building components contract from the cold and pull away from one another. On the other hand, sealants applied in the winter may become overcompressed in the summer when the building components expand with the heat and push toward one another. It is this overcompression that causes the sealant to protrude from the joint.

The development of modern sealants parallels the development of paints (see pp. 39–41). Before 1950, all sealants were plain caulking, made out of oil and powdered chalk. This caulking needed weather protection itself, and most often was covered with a coat of paint. Around 1950, latex caulks became very popular, because of their ease of cleanup. They are still used today, mostly for such tasks as sealing around doors and windows, and sealing minor cracks in concrete.

Elastomeric sealants are used in larger buildings for sealing curtain walls and for control joints in concrete, bricks, and steel. Elastomeric sealants should not be painted—they need to move in order to do their intended jobs.

In addition to gunnable sealants, there are solid types of sealants that are placed in the seams of buildings. Solid sealants are usually made of rubberlike plastic, and can take the form of gaskets or tapes. Like the soft gray yuck, they should be left in place.

Exterior building panels, such as the ones shown, sometimes appear on closer examination to be stuck together with extraneous gray yuck. Do not remove! In the building illustrated, one would find the yuck in the horizontal and vertical joints (emphasized).

WHO WAS LOUIS I. KAHN?

"Ask the brick what it wants to be" are the words of Louis I. Kahn (1901–1974), an immigrant from Russia at the age of four to Philadelphia, which became his lifelong home. While there is no evidence that he actually walked around interrogating building components, his architecture in form and massing consistently revealed the character of the material used.

Kahn was chief critic at Yale from 1948 to 1957, and then teacher at the University of Pennsylvania, his alma mater. He built on the philosophies

of the modern movement, and coined the concept of "servant and served space," clearly separating occupied areas of a building from mechanical and circulation areas. Some of his most noteworthy buildings included the Salk Institute in La Jolla, California (1965), the Library at the Exeter Academy in New Hampshire (1972), Unitarian Church in Rochester, New York (1969), and the Art Gallery at Yale (1953). Kahn was an admirer of India and did planning and building work there that includes the Institute of Management at Ahmedabad (1974).

Kahn's skill in the use and control of natural light perhaps is best exemplified through the Kimbell Art Museum in Fort Worth, Texas (1972).

Louis I. Kahn did not actually converse with building materials, but he made them speak eloquently, as evidenced by his design of the Unitarian Church in Rochester, New York, built in 1969.

WHO WAS LOUIS HENRI SULLIVAN?

Louis Henri Sullivan (1856–1924) espoused an architecture that was uniquely American—democratic, pragmatic, and proudly beautiful. Like Daniel Burnham (see pp. 136–137), he began his career in the Chicago office of William LeBaron Jenney. With partner Dankmar Adler, the firm of Admar and Sullivan designed some 180 buildings, many in Chicago. Admar's talent in acoustic and mechanical design, coupled with Sullivan's artistic genius, produced unmatched theater design, most notably for the Chicago Auditorium (the largest in the world in 1890 when it was built). The firm was also known for its "skyscraper design"—symbol of the new American building—through the ten-story Wainwright Building in St. Louis, the Chicago Stock Exchange (1893), and the Guaranty Building in Buffalo (1894).

In 1896 Sullivan published an essay entitled, "The Tall Office Building Artistically Considered," in which he described the new architectural phenomenon: "It must be every inch a proud and soaring thing, rising in sheer exultation." He also said, "Where function does not change, form does not change . . . the pervading law of all things . . . form ever follows function. That is the law."

After his split with Adler in 1985, Sullivan did mostly minor works, including some small but exquisite banks. Problems of arrogance, alcohol, and arguments with most of the rest of the architectural profession ruined his reputation and drove clients away. Often living in abject poverty, he turned to writing, and his *Kindergarten Chats* (a series of fictional conversations between architectural master and apprentice), first published as a series of magazine articles in 1901 and 1902, and then in book form in 1934, are still read widely by architecture students. *A System of Architectural Ornament* and *Autobiography of an Idea* (which covered his life only until 1893) was published in 1924 at the time of his death. A profession that could not forgive the man his arrogance during his life still sings his praises some seventy years since his death. Sullivan's magnificent architecture, of course, has outlived both naysayers and supporters.

Louis Sullivan formed the 1904 Guaranty Building in Buffalo, New York, to perform the function of a tall office building, artistically considered.

47

CHAPTER TWO STRUCTURES AND BUILDING SYSTEMS

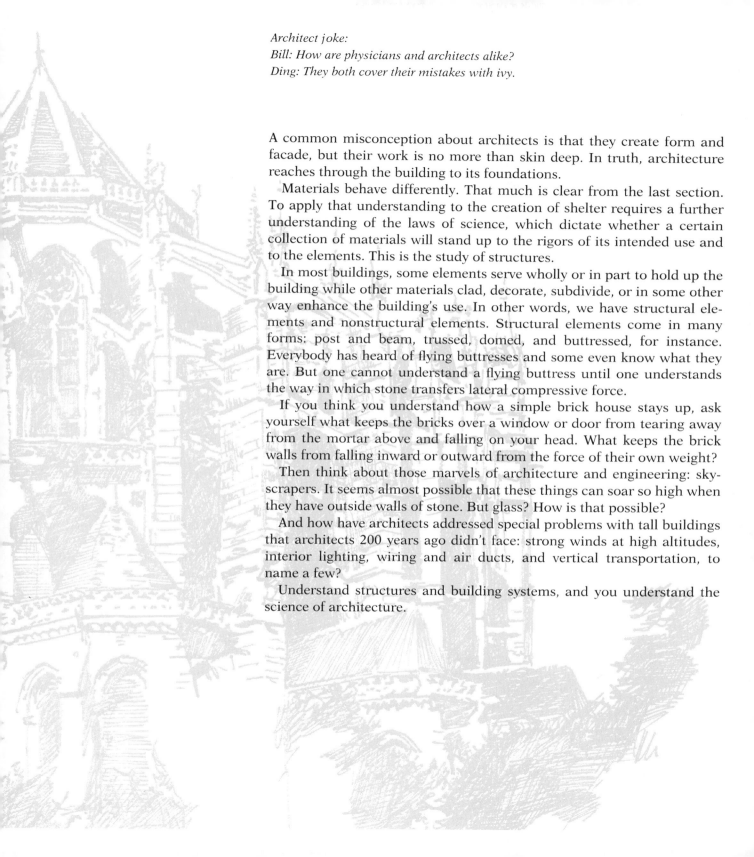

Architect joke:
Bill: How are physicians and architects alike?
Ding: They both cover their mistakes with ivy.

A common misconception about architects is that they create form and facade, but their work is no more than skin deep. In truth, architecture reaches through the building to its foundations.

Materials behave differently. That much is clear from the last section. To apply that understanding to the creation of shelter requires a further understanding of the laws of science, which dictate whether a certain collection of materials will stand up to the rigors of its intended use and to the elements. This is the study of structures.

In most buildings, some elements serve wholly or in part to hold up the building while other materials clad, decorate, subdivide, or in some other way enhance the building's use. In other words, we have structural elements and nonstructural elements. Structural elements come in many forms: post and beam, trussed, domed, and buttressed, for instance. Everybody has heard of flying buttresses and some even know what they are. But one cannot understand a flying buttress until one understands the way in which stone transfers lateral compressive force.

If you think you understand how a simple brick house stays up, ask yourself what keeps the bricks over a window or door from tearing away from the mortar above and falling on your head. What keeps the brick walls from falling inward or outward from the force of their own weight?

Then think about those marvels of architecture and engineering: sky-scrapers. It seems almost possible that these things can soar so high when they have outside walls of stone. But glass? How is that possible?

And how have architects addressed special problems with tall buildings that architects 200 years ago didn't face: strong winds at high altitudes, interior lighting, wiring and air ducts, and vertical transportation, to name a few?

Understand structures and building systems, and you understand the science of architecture.

WHAT IS THE DIFFERENCE BETWEEN STRUCTURAL/ NONSTRUCTURAL AND BEARING/ NONBEARING?

A bearing member is always structural, but a structural member is not always bearing. A structural member is any part of a building that helps hold up the building. Posts, columns, beams, floors, and some walls and roofs are structural because they hold one another together. At the same time, they hold in place all the nonstructural parts of the building—curtain walls, windows, roof topping, and so on—that make it comfortable, light filled, and accessible.

A bearing member, on the other hand, is more narrowly defined as a support for load, such as a beam or joist. The difference between bearing and nonbearing structural components is fairly simple. One provides support for its vertical load, and the other provides load resistance in some other direction, a tie bar or a hanger, for example.

Walls provide a good example of the differences among the terms structural, nonstructural, bearing, and nonbearing. A bearing wall is one that carries at least part of the weight of the building above it. So a bearing wall is always a structural component of the building. Some buildings, especially those built where earthquakes are a hazard, have what are called *shear walls*, which stiffen the building against side-to-side motion. Sometimes shear walls are load bearing, but not always. A wall that doesn't support weight, but is designed to resist side-to-side movement is a nonbearing, structural wall. And suppose a wall neither supports weight nor resists shear forces. Suppose it is like a good number of the walls in your home or in office buildings, and consists of little more than a couple of pieces of sheetrock held up by two-by-fours or thinly rolled steel studs. At the very least, the wall defines the boundaries of rooms or offices and creates acoustic and visual privacy. So the wall is functional. Put up wallpaper and a few pictures, and it's decorative too. But it's neither load bearing nor structural.

There is another difference that is the source of much design consideration—that is, the differences among structure, function, and decoration, and the integration of the three. For example, a structural element may also be functional (such as a column that serves as a kiosk) and decorative (the same column with carved cherubs). Cathedrals, with beautifully carved stonework forming long processional naves and congregational apses, often are cited as the most perfect integration of form, structure, and function ever conceived.

The stone structural bearing walls of a cathedral have been called the most perfect integration of form, structure, and function.

WHAT IS POST AND BEAM CONSTRUCTION?

Architecture is the making of space, and that involves working in three dimensions. One of the simplest, cheapest, and most common ways to build the common denominators of enclosing three-dimensional space—a floor, walls, and a roof—is with wood post and beam construction. *Posts* (or columns) are the vertical members, and the beams are the horizontal members. Post and beam buildings carry the weight of their structural components (and the weight of the objects and people within them) by bearing on one another. That is, the weight of the roof and beams is carried by the posts down to the foundation and into mother earth.

The Parthenon illustrates that "post and beam" literally means any kind of vertical post (such as these columns) supporting any kind of horizontal beam (even beams made of stone).

52

The fancy, architectural name for this kind of construction employing any type of material is *trabeated* (from the Latin word for beam), meaning that openings in the building are spanned by beams, as opposed to arches (see pp. 60–61). We've been building this way for a long time—the Parthenon is one example.

The structural concept translates easily to wood: heavy wood posts to hold up wood beams. Today's version, called "wood light frame construction," was invented in Chicago by an engineer and builder named George Washington Snow in the 1830s. Because of the new preponderance of sawmills and machine-made nails at the time, he was able to create a lightweight, cheaper method of building by replacing commonly used heavy wood posts with lighter wood studs (see pp. 27–28), floor beams with joists (see pp. 54–55), and roof beams with rafters (lightweight, diagonally positioned beams). All components could now be handled by one or two workers, and the components' lightness and thinness allowed them to be nailed together, replacing expensive and time-consuming methods of traditional joinery.

Snow's system of building was termed *balloon framing* by his detractors, who thought it too light and flimsy to catch on. The name has stuck to this day; no longer with insulting overtones. However, most light wood framing today is of the type called *western* or *platform* framing, and differs from balloon framing in one significant aspect. In balloon framing for a two-story building, the studs are two stories tall, extending from the roof to the foundation. In platform framing, the studs extend only from one floor level to the next, and rest on the top of the floor. These shorter studs are easier to handle, and the connections between studs and floors eliminate paths for fires.

WHY ARE TRUSSES AND
JOISTS SHAPED THE WAY THEY
ARE—WITH HORIZONTAL TOPS
AND BOTTOMS, AND DIAGONAL
PIECES AS CONNECTORS?

Consider first the job that trusses have to perform—they are designed to carry a vertical load in the the same way that a beam does. When a beam is loaded with evenly distributed weight, it bends. Often, the bending is slight, but it is enough to make the top of the beam slightly shorter and the bottom of the sagging beam slightly longer. This puts the top in compression and the bottom in tension. A steel beam is shaped like an "I" so that its heavy flanges, which carry most of the load, are connected by a thin web, equivalent to the vertical stroke of the "I." A truss is designed in the same way. It has heavier horizontal members (called the chords) to take tension and compression, and smaller diagonals (called web members) in the middle. These middle members are placed diagonally simply because that is a more efficient way of transferring the load (a triangle is the most stable flat shape, and diagonal web members form a series of triangles). Some trusses (called *vierendeel trusses,* after their inventor) do use vertical web members.

Having less material in the center where it is not really needed allows trusses to be manufactured of less material. This makes them lighter and therefore easier to install. Less material in a truss also means less weight in the overall building, and, of course, less expense during manufacture.

You will notice, if you look closely at a steel truss, that the top chord is attached to the columns on either end, but the bottom chord is slightly shorter than the top one, and its ends are not connected to the columns at all. This is because the weight of the load above is creating compression in the top chord, which passes through the diagonal struts to become tension in the bottom chord. As long as the bottom chord can withstand the stretching force, it is working. It doesn't have to be connected to the column.

Trusses and joists simply function as beams with "holes," where material is not needed to carry the structural weight.

What is a flying buttress?

On the sides of stone cathedrals you often see a series of ornate piers connected at the top to the cathedral exterior with arched masonry bridges. That is a flying buttress. More interesting than what a flying buttress is, though, is what it does.

First, it's important to know the state of construction at the time cathedral building flourished. It was during the time of the Holy Roman Empire, when the Catholic Church held considerable sway in Europe, that cathedral construction became a matter of high art and science. In the Middle Ages, cathedrals built of stone—even with arches and domes to add ornamental interest—were heavy, dark, cumbersome buildings. The Gothic cathedrals that followed, however, show an attempt to make the church a breathtakingly welcome place of gathering through the use of light and openness. Still building with stone and depending on its structural strength in compression, Gothic cathedral builders were able to create interior spaces over 150 feet high with great expanses of stained glass windows piercing the structural integrity of the walls. Because of the windows, the walls couldn't hold themselves and the weight of the roof structure too, so something else had to. The roof consisted of struc-

Gothic cathedrals are the bailiwick of flying buttresses, which provide lateral support for the massive stone walls, as shown in the Cathedral at LeMans, completed in 1217.

56

tural ribs (intricately combined heavy stone arches) that carried the weight of the roof outward to the sides of the building.

Think of throwing a ball outward. The path it traces on the way to the ground looks like an arch. That is also the path a force takes when it is thrust outward, beyond the cathedral walls (natural forces follow the path of least resistance). By putting compressive-strong stone along those lines of compressive force, the weight of the roof is transferred to the heavy, hard-to-move exterior piers, which, in turn, carry the load to the ground.

Stone can easily take the compressive forces this kind of arrangement puts on it. But a problem with this sort of creative manipulation of forces is that the structural elements—the stones—depend on one another to stay in place. If you dislodge just a few stones in the right places, the entire section of the building is likely to fall down. Still, the system can be quite stable, as is evident from the length of time the medieval cathedrals have been standing. It just so happens that it is very difficult to dislodge one of those stones.

Put your arms over your head and press against a wall with your hands. Presto—you're a flying buttress!

HOW DOES A DOME WORK?

The visual impact is the first thing most people notice about a dome. Appearing unassuming, even diminutive, from the outside, domes—even small ones—create an optical illusion of immensity when seen from inside. Without corners and ceiling-to-wall connections which we usually see inside a room, and which we subconsciously use to gauge the room's boundaries, a dome can easily be made, with paint and light, to look like the limitless heavens—a fact that has made them popular forms for churches, capitols, and planetarium labs.

Domes are more than aesthetic elements. A dome is also one of the most practical ways of covering a large space. This seamless blending of visual appeal and structural elegance inspired engineer and author Mario Salvadori to call the dome "the greatest architectural and structural achievement of mankind in over 2,000 years of spiritual and technological development."

Domes have been made of many materials—such as stone, brick, tile, concrete, plastic, and metal—and they take many shapes and sizes. They all work on the same general principle, which is similar to that of the arch. The weight at the top presses down along a semicircular path to the ground. As long as the building material is strong enough to withstand the compressive force from above, the force acts to hold the shape of the dome. The shape is so stable that it is possible to build a dome with carefully shaped blocks without mortar. The weight of the blocks above holds in place the blocks below. An igloo is an example.

Michelangelo's Dome of St. Peter's Cathedral, completed in 1564, forms one of Rome's most beloved landmarks.

Fine, but how does all this work? It is the monolithic action of the dome as a shell that makes it work the way it does, and which makes a dome much different from an arch. Forces radiate from the top downward through a dome along meridians (much like the longitudinal lines of a globe). You can think of these meridians as arch segments. Remember, though, that an arch needs a tie-bar or buttressing to keep the two ends from kicking outward. This tendency is significantly less in a dome because it is a continuous shell that has parallel strength holding in its girth (something like the strength hoops give to a barrel).

The thickness of the dome shell (measured as a ratio to the radius of the dome's hemisphere) can be about ten times less than the ratio of the thickness of an arch to its semicircle. In fact, domes are the most material-efficient structural shapes in building construction.

Although domes use materials efficiently, their construction can be cumbersome and inefficient. The dome is a classic building form largely because it works well with compressively strong masonry. The complication, though, is that a dome only works to hold itself up when it is a complete shell. To keep the incomplete dome from falling in during construction, masons used heavy timber scaffolding. This process, called *centering*, required that large portions of the dome be supported from the inside. The process used so much timber and was so cumbersome that it restricted the practical size for domes to around 150 feet in diameter.

These days, stone has become too expensive for use as a general building material. And, being a natural material, its properties are hard for engineers to calculate within the margins of error required today for the sake of building economics. So, large stone-looking domes built over the last few decades are more than likely made of steel-reinforced concrete.

Other materials—mostly wood, plastic, and metal—also make workable and affordable domes. Plywood and plastic can be molded into a single-piece shell, but manufacturing limitations keep such shells down to a dozen or so feet in diameter at most. Plastic bubbles have become quite common in skylights. One early use of plastic bubbles, dating back to World War II, was for cockpit canopies on warplanes. For larger domes, plastic or wood ribs form the skeleton of the dome, while plywood or plastic membranes enclose it.

Steel domes are commonly made of such an infill shell wrapped over reinforced ribs. The steel reinforcement may or may not be a dome itself. It may be a truss covered with thinly cut (and therefore nonstructural) stone, or, as is the case with shopping malls and hotel lobbies, a frame of steel studs may be covered by wire mesh on which plaster is smeared (the end product winds up looking a lot like stone). With such thin and—relative to solid stone—lightweight domes, engineers have to take into account forces that didn't concern masons of old. As weight goes down, the relative effect of wind, ground motion, and so on go up, which requires calculating for cross bracing and tie-downs.

How do bricks over doors and windows stay in place?

Try stacking sugar cubes some time, and see if you can make an opening, like a window, that is at least one sugar cube wide. After a while, you'll start to appreciate that doors and windows are weak spots in a brick wall. You might suppose that the mortar in a brick wall gives the mason an advantage over your typical sugar cube stacker, but that's not actually so. Mortar has enough strength to keep a wall in place, but most of its strength is compressive. You can put a lot of weight on it and it won't squash. However, mortar is very weak when it comes to tensile strength. A child could snap in two the thin strip of mortar that goes between each pair of courses of bricks. So if the brick above a door or window is supported only by the mortar, the weight of the wall above will make the bricks above an opening sag. The force—considerably more than a child could exert—will snap mortar and brick alike, cracks will form, and more than likely the brick wall will fall.

So if it isn't the mortar, what holds up the bricks over a window or door? There are three basic ways that an opening can be made without having the wall above fall down. If, when stacking sugar cubes, you weren't too concerned that your wall opening had square corners, you might figure out that by stacking cubes in an overlapping pattern that gradually narrows the opening as the brick courses ascend, you've got a rough opening. In masonry, such an arrangement is called a *corbeled*

One way to hold bricks in place over an opening is to arrange them in an arch.

60

opening. In each course, the end brick (the one that extends into the window or door opening) must project no more than one third of its length to safely support the load above. In brick walls, as with sugar cubes, corbels create odd-shaped openings that are difficult to fill with standard-shaped windows and doors. That is why you don't see them used very often.

The second way to bridge the gap over a wall opening—and one that is much more common than corbels—is to arrange bricks in an arch. Bricks and stone are great materials for arches because in an arch, the weight above the opening is pushing the bricks in the arch together rather than trying to tear them apart. The key to getting this to work is the top stone of the arch (that's why it's called the *keystone*).

Look at an arched opening sometime and notice that either the bricks ascending on each side, or the mortar joints between them, are somewhat wedge shaped, and become more so toward the top. The mortar on each side of the keystone has the largest angle of all in the arch and, as you can see, can't fall because it is wedged in place by the weight of the wall above. If you think of the weight of the wall as thrust (directional force), you can see in a brick arch that the thrust will follow down each side of the arch to the wall on either side of the opening. That outward force is called lateral thrust. Since an arch directs the weight above the wall opening sideways into the wall beside it, the wall beside an arch has to be strong enough to take the extra force. That's why sometimes you see that a wall is built so that it's thicker around an arched opening.

Arches can be built out of common, rectangular bricks, in which case they are called rough arches. Or, arches can be built out of specially shaped bricks called *voussoirs*, which follow the curve of the arch. Arches can take a variety of forms, the shape of which is often dictated by the architectural style of the building (see pp. 169–170). One can even get a flat arch, which creates a window with squared corners.

When building an arch, workers have to build a scaffold to hold the bricks up until the keystone is put in place (an arch only works when it's complete). An easier way to bridge a wall opening is the third, and probably most common, way that bricks stay in place over a window or door: A *lintel* is a beam that carries the weight of the masonry above and transfers that weight to the wall on either side of the opening. The result is an opening with squared corners that can be capped and built over without too much special consideration.

A lintel is easy to see if it is a horizontal beam of stone or concrete. Sometimes you have to look closely to see a lintel, for instance when it is a thin piece of steel holding up the bricks. When bricks appear to run unsupported directly over an opening, the lintel is hidden inside the wall, created from a steel reinforcing bar buried within the brickwork. If there is a course of vertical bricks over a door or window, chances are very good that a steel rod is doing the work of holding them in place.

What are those iron stars that often appear on the sides of old brick buildings?

They are the ends of metal bars, probably wrought iron, that extend through the building (hidden within a ceiling or floor, or sometimes exposed in the rafters) from one outside surface to the opposite one. Builders used these steel bars in tension to keep the outside walls of multistory brick buildings from falling outward.

These tie-rods, as they are called, are a simple way to resist overturning force. A wall can be seen to work like a huge hinge that wants to bend at its connection to the ground. When the wind blows, for instance, the overturning force at the ground (which is a "moment" force) gets proportionately greater as the wall gets higher (moment at a hinge equals force times the distance of the force from the hinge).

When you put four walls together to make a building, they tend to hold themselves together at the corners, depending on the strength of the building material. Masonry is strong in compression, so the corners help a lot to keep the walls from falling inward. The joists, flooring, and cross walls within the building act as internal bracing, helping even more to keep the walls from falling in.

But masonry is weak in tension, so the corners don't help much in keeping the four walls of a multistory building from falling outward. Moreover, a roof, especially a pitched roof, is likely to add to the outward push on the exterior walls. Short of buttressing the outsides of the walls with heavy, hard-to-push-over masonry piers, there isn't any way of building a tall brick structure without help from some other material—usually wood or metal—which can reinforce the masonry in tension. Because wrought iron could do the same work as wood, yet take up much less room doing it, tie-rods became the tension reinforcement of choice in the eighteenth century whenever designers wanted to get more usable space by using less bulky structures.

A tie-rod extends through the outside walls on each side of a building where the bar ends are attached to the stars, which are the parts that actually hold the wall in. Although other shapes have been used, the star seems to be the most popular, perhaps because it is an efficient, mass-producible shape for spreading the force of the steel against enough brick area to prevent punch shear. In addition, of course, stars look nice. In the absence of such a structure, the end of the tie-rod might break through the wall instead of holding it up.

Iron stars as shown on the sides of this old brick building look decorative but have a structural function.

WHAT IS A TENSION STRUCTURE?

Just as your neck muscles feel stretched when you have a "tension" headache, a building component is stretched when it is in tension. Tension in a building component is a reaction to an externally applied force. At a molecular level, it is an action that tends to separate adjacent particles of a material. String a clothesline between two poles, hang on the line (in other words, act like a force) and you will put the line in tension. The ability of a structural material to withstand stretching forces is called its tensile strength. Steel has a very high tensile strength, while concrete has a low tensile strength.

One common and readily visible type of tension structure is the cable-suspended bridge, examples of which are the Golden Gate in San Francisco (1937) and the Verrazano-Narrows in New York (1964). The deck of the bridge and the weight of the cars and trucks driving over it (the force) are supported by cables (in tension) attached to the masts, which in turn carry the force down to the foundations. Deceptively slender-looking, tension cables are made up of numerous wire strands bundled together. One of the most famous cable-suspended bridges, the Brooklyn Bridge (1883), has cables close to 16 inches in diameter, each made of over 5,000 wires wrapped in a coated-wire spiral.

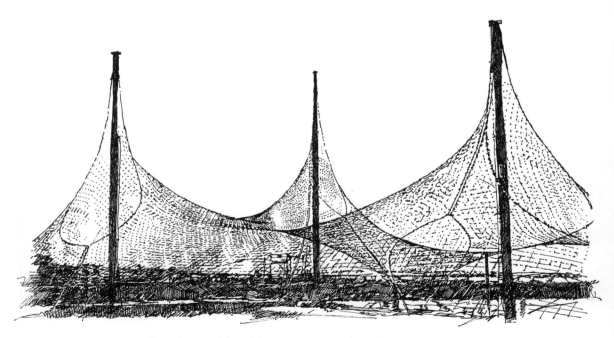

Structures with cables are supported in "tension," that is, by cables stretched or pulled tight.

Cables holding up roof structures form another type of tension structure, ranging in scale from a boy scout's blanket over a clothesline to the soaring stadiums that cover tens of thousands of square feet. Large tension structures can be covered with fabric that itself is stretched into tension to prevent fluttering. One of the largest of these tent structures is Frei Otto's Munich Olympic Stadium built in 1972, which covered 18 acres. Another popular type of cable structure roof, one that can span hundreds of feet, is called a tension ring structure. One example is the roof of Madison Square Garden in New York City. In this type of roof structure, radial cables stretch from an outer perimeter ring, which is supported on a wall or on columns, to a free-hanging inner ring that is both smaller in diameter and lower in height. This arrangement gives the roof a dish shape. The cables are then topped with concrete slabs, which puts them in tension. The cables in turn pull the fibers of the inner tension ring outward, placing it, of course, in tension. The cables pull the fibers of the outer compression ring inward, squashing them together and placing the ring in compression. Both the cables and the tension ring are constructed of steel because of its high tensile strength, while the compression can be of steel or concrete.

HOW DO FABRIC ROOFS
STAND UP?

Many of them are huge tents, supported in the same method as the blanket strung over the clothesline to create a backyard tent (see pp. 64–65). The cables that form the structural support are stretched (placed in tension) until they are rigid. For the tent in the backyard, we would also want to make the fabric rigid, maybe by driving stakes into the ground and fastening the blanket tight to the stakes. Large, fabric tension roofs work on the same principle: The fabric is placed in tension and becomes rigid and therefore a more satisfactory roof, in terms of keeping out rain, not fluttering in the wind, and not drooping on our heads.

While tent structures are as old as the hills, a newer type of fabric structure, gaining popularity rapidly, is supported by air. Like balloons, air-supported structures are held up by a positive internal pressure. In the case of buildings, a steady flow of air constantly supplied by large fans creates the higher pressure inside. You don't have to worry about such a building collapsing over your head—air-supported structures have an emergency power backup for the fans. And even if the backup power failed, backup cables would hold the fabric up if the air went off. (And,

The U.S. Pavilion in Osaka, Japan (by architect Davis Brody), sports a fabric roof that is held up by cables.

lest you do not like the concept of air as a structural material in the first place, consider the reminder of engineer Mario Salvadori: What's holding up the tires that are holding up the car you drive everyday?)

Air-supported structures can be very flexible in the amount of structural support they provide. For instance, if there is a heavy snowfall, the air pressure can be increased to support the extra load of the snow. Alternatively, the air supplied by the fans can be heated to melt the snow.

All kinds of fabric roofs can be used to create large expanses of column-free indoor space, which is why they are popular for stadiums, sport events (such as tennis and swimming pools), and showrooms. Their other useful characteristics include light weight and thinness, which make them relatively easy to build and repair. Translucency to light allows natural daylight to be spread evenly across a large interior area.

Tension roofs usually are made of a fiberglass (or fiberglasslike) material covered with a fire-, water-, and ultraviolet-resistant coating, such as Teflon. Their life span is about twenty years, at which point the material has to be replaced.

How are steel frames put together?

Because much of our firsthand experience with structure is with housing, we are familiar with the nailing of wood construction and the mortaring of bricks. Steel frames, for the most part covered over in larger, commercial buildings, are more mysterious. When you consider that the steel frame is a variation of a simple post and beam system, it doesn't seem so complicated. In fact, there are only three ways of attaching steel to steel.

Riveting is the oldest method of fastening two steel members. A rivet is a short pin that has a pointed end and a head end (like a very short, fat nail). The rivet is heated white-hot, then its pointed end is placed through holes in both pieces of steel to be attached; then it is hammered flat so that it forms a second head. When the rivet cools, it shrinks and pulls the two pieces of steel closer together. Placing hot rivets is dangerous work, and this method has been supplanted by other methods. (Author Ayn Rand had the hero of *The Fountainhead*, Howard Roark, working as a rivet catcher on high-steel buildings before he became an architect, in order to illustrate the true metal of the man.)

Bolting is the most common method of joining steel members, because it is the easiest and quickest method, and can be performed on the building site under any weather conditions. A bolt is placed between holes in the two pieces of steel to be joined, and tightened (usually with a specially calibrated wrench) to get exactly the right fit. (If the bolt is too loose, the connection will be weak. If it is too tight, the bolt may snap under the pressure.)

Welding is the third major method of connecting steel members. Welding connections can be accomplished either by melting portions of the two steel pieces to be joined and pressing them together, or by adding molten steel between the two pieces, which acts like a glue. The advantage to welding is that the two pieces of steel act monolithically to resist structural forces. It is not uncommon for bolting and welding both to be used for the fastening of steel members. For instance, two steel beams may be bolted (an easier task) and held by the bolts for welding, which is a more complicated and precise operation to accomplish on site.

This illustration shows the various ways steel frames can be put together.

How do glass buildings with no visible frames stand up?

You've seen them in any urban center and in almost every suburb—those boxes with large, smooth expanses of glass that seem to float in the air without any means of support. This is a new type of technology called structural silicone glazing, and it is literally "glued on glass." The glue, which is a sealant made of silicone, is a structural material that transfers the load (the weight) of the glass panels to a backup frame behind the glass facade. (For a discussion of structural versus nonstructural materials, see pp. 50–51). The glass walls that show no means of support from the outside are called four-sided systems, because each glass panel is attached on all four edges to the frame with silicone. This type of system is referred to in the trade as *total wall* or *stopless* glazing.

Glass facades on which you can see the frame, either as horizontal or vertical bands, are two-sided systems, with one pair of opposing edges glued with silicone onto adjacent pieces of glass, and the other pair of edges resting in pockets in the exposed (usually aluminum) frame. This type of silicone glazing system is called *strip glazing*.

Almost any kind of glass can be used in a structural silicone glazing system, which accounts for the great visual variety among these types of buildings. Their one common feature is the silicone that is used for attachment—to date, it is the only material that has the right characteristics for the job. Not only must it be strong enough to support the weight of the glass, it must also be flexible enough to transfer the unpredictable force of the wind hitting the glass facade back to the frame. In some cases, it does double duty as a weather seal, keeping wind and water from seeping into the building.

Another popular type of glass system that has large, "floating" panels of glass and no metal frame is the *fin system*, which uses glass mullion "fins" perpendicular to the glass panels to stabilize the facade. If the panels are more than one story tall, they are fastened together with metal clips at their edges. Although structural in the sense that they support their own weight, fin systems do not rely on their sealants for structural support, so cannot be classified as glued-on glass.

Glass buildings with no visible frames have exterior "glued on glass" with support frames behind it.

Is it dangerous if a tall building sways?

Say you're on an upper floor of a sixty- or seventy-story building, and you have an uncomfortable feeling of instability. Maybe it's a pencil that keeps rolling off the desk, or that you notice that, when you sit still and line up the window sill with a neighboring building, the orientation shifts ever so slightly. You suddenly realize you're 900 feet up in a building that is moving—some buildings can move 50 feet in 20 seconds—and your first instinct is to grab for the carpeting and hold on. That's a rational fear, actually, but an unfounded one all the same. The fact is, tall buildings sway—it's the nature of the structural systems used to scrape the sky.

For a building to get as far off the ground as skyscrapers do, they need designs that use as little material as possible. The more weight per foot of building, the larger the structure must be to hold itself up. Furthermore, the more material necessary, the more expensive the building. So building designers have a lot of incentive to minimize weight and material. And they have been successful. With cross bracing, huge trusses, and multiple and bundled structural cores, architects and engineers have been able to send extraordinarily thin and fragile-looking buildings soaring through the clouds. They are as sure as their calculation and safety factors allow them to be that the buildings won't fall, even though winds push quite hard at skyscraper heights.

Typically, the engineers brace the building to withstand the wind that is specified in the local building code and include a safety factor (multiplying by two, for instance) based on the type of building. But even within the jurisdiction of a local building code, there are microclimatic conditions that might require special design consideration. There are factors other than wind, too. Lying within a high-risk earthquake zone has become a major factor, especially with the public attention to the disasters in Los Angeles, Mexico City, Armenia, and San Francisco over recent years. There are many more mundane sources of building movement, as well. Having a subway running beneath a building, for example, creates a lot of vibration. While that doesn't often threaten the integrity of the building structure, it can wreak havoc with sensitive equipment in a lab or hospital.

When special conditions exist, designers often resort to special testing. Laboratories are widely available, often through university or government facilities, for conducting wind tunnel tests on building scale models. With scale models of the proposed building's surroundings—geographic and man-made—and scaled-down wind speeds, scientists use force sensors and smoke to tell fairly accurately how the real building will behave on its site. Computerized simulations are also widely possible, and fairly accurate, with the boom in computer-aided design systems.

To get the most accurate results, though, one needs to test a full-scale

Tall buildings, such as New York's Seagram Building by Mies van der Rohe and Philip Johnson, are built to sway flexibly in the wind instead of snapping.

73

mockup. This often means constructing an expensive, and often very large, piece of the building in a special facility (such facilities are scarce) where it will be pushed, pulled, probed, and pummeled to pieces. Obviously, this is a strategy only for very special cases. But, if the building owner is likely to save a lot of money avoiding costly construction mistakes, he or she can spend a lot of money destroying a wildly expensive mockup, and still end up saving bucks in the long run.

But even with all the calculating and testing to make sure a skyscraper won't fall, it is still going to sway in the wind—it's simply too expensive to stiffen a tall building enough that it doesn't sway. In moderate amounts, that is all right. Sway is a design problem, however, if building occupants are uncomfortable or if it affects equipment necessary to the building's function. In these cases, the designer overcomes building sway most often by stiffening the frame—usually by adding more steel or concrete, but also possibly by reconfiguring the structure.

But remember, the designer always strives to minimize weight and quantity of material, especially in tall buildings. To minimize sway and material quantity, some strategies for dampening building movement use finesse over brute strength. A very sophisticated one, first contrived in the 1970s by engineer William LeMessurier for the Citicorp Building in New York City, is the tuned mass damper. It consists of a large lead weight floating on a skim of oil so it can be pushed about by a computer-controlled motor. As the building sways, the computer shifts the lead weight to counteract the swaying movement. (Think of the playground swing. If you pump your legs with the swing, you go higher. Pump your legs against the swing's motion, and you slow down.)

Another strategy is to put energy-absorbing isolation on the base columns or structural connections. With base isolation, each column bears at ground level on a base isolator made of layers of hard rubber and lead, often with a steel core. The base isolator is strong enough in compression to hold up the building, yet is more ductile than the steel column alone. Because the isolator bends a little when wind or ground motion moves the building, it absorbs energy that otherwise would make the building sway. The same principle can be applied to all the bolted joints in a steel frame. By putting some kind of elastomer—something that accommodates movement (like rubber), then returns to its original shape—between bolted connections, tests have shown that an entire building frame can act to dampen building vibration and sway. Although base isolation has become a somewhat common building technology, frame-connection isolation is still in the developmental stages.

WHAT IS A SPACE FRAME AND HOW DOES IT WORK?

Given that a building structure's purpose is to resist forces such as gravity, wind, thermal expansion and contraction, and sometimes earthquakes, it has to resist forces in all directions. So, what if you had a material that could resist tension as well as compression and you made bars or tubes out of it? Then, maybe, if you put them together in the right way, you could devise a lightweight, open structure where all of the bars acted to resist force applied from any direction. Then you could make a building that held itself up as well as one made of bricks or concrete, but which was more airy and open than a steel-frame building.

The Jacob Javits Convention Center in New York City, designed by I. M. Pei & Partners, has a space frame structure.

That was the way Buckminster Fuller's thoughts were heading when he devised the "geodesic/tensegrity" structure in 1927. He explained the concept with the word "synergy," the phenomenon of the action of the whole being greater than the sum of its operating parts.

A *space frame* is a three-dimensional structure (it resists force in any direction). Fuller, with his *geodesic dome*, proved that the space-frame principle worked, but accurate calculation of how well it worked was too complicated for calculators of the time. Because thousands of pieces work together as individual force resistors, the mathematics necessary to calculate what was happening where was well beyond the scope of human ability, and computers couldn't calculate quickly enough to crack the space-frame nut until the 1960s. And it wasn't until the 1980s that powerful computers were inexpensive enough to make space-frame calculations (called *finite analysis*) a common phenomenon.

As it turns out, with the increasing ease and accuracy of complex mathematics figured on machines, space frames are likely to become more and more common as architects strive to achieve more drama with their designs and owners strive to achieve more economy with their buildings. Space frames are no longer limited to dome shapes. With columns, box girders, and flat trusses also possible, building shape has never been more flexible.

WHY DO SO MANY BUILDINGS TODAY HAVE WINDOWS THAT DON'T OPEN?

It's good to be able to open a window on a nice day and feel the fresh outdoor breeze streaming through. Everybody likes that. So it may seem a bit strange that so many buildings have windows that cannot be opened at all. They let light in and let people look out at the world, but that's it. A major reason for having fixed windows in buildings is air conditioning. If the air conditioners are on in a building, you want as much of the cool air to stay inside as possible. Windows that can be left open often are, and even in a medium-size building, leakage from insufficiently sealed windows can be sizable. Fixed windows are more weathertight than operable windows, and, barring a catastrophe, they're bound to be closed. So for the sake of saving air-conditioning energy, fixed windows in medium-size and larger buildings make simple economic sense.

Increased energy efficiency in windows also comes through various glass coatings that let in cool light in the visible spectrum but control passage of radiant heat through double-glazing. The dead-air space between the glass in a double-paned window gives some insulation value. (Windows are notoriously bad for letting heat in or out, which is why we have heavy drapes, reflective window blinds, and shady roof overhangs.)

Quite often, the double-glazed windows are made of specially coated glass, sometimes filled with an inert gas—such as argon—that provides more insulation than air. All this is expensive, and because double-glazed windows are heavy and bulky, making them operable would also be expensive. Since the building operator probably wants to keep all the windows closed all the time anyway, there isn't much incentive for the designer to go out of the way to work in operable windows.

Another reason has more to do specifically with windows in high-rise buildings. The wind is so strong at the tops of tall buildings that the windows have to be pretty much airtight. The wind flows much more strongly at the heights achievable even with moderately tall buildings. The real numbers fluctuate from place to place, but it's not too unusual for an architect to have to design windows that withstand 100-mile-per-hour (mph) winds. For instance, one of the major regional building codes requires that in those areas (and much of the United States falls in this category) where the wind has a .02 probability (meaning about once every fifty years) of blowing at 70 mph at 30 feet, the designer needs to plan for a windspeed at 150 feet of more than 105 mph.

Wind at such high velocity does some unusual things. Air pressure builds up on the windward side, as one might suspect. But as one might not expect, air pressure goes down on the sides, top, and back—a little at the sides of a cube-shaped building, but a lot at the top and back side. When the air pressure goes down outside the building but stays the same

*I. M. Pei's John Hancock in Boston
sports story upon story of reflective (but
unopenable) glass windows.*

inside the building, a lot of force pushes at the windows from the inside. Directions and intensities of wind forces can change instantly when a window is opened. So windows subject to beatings by high winds have to be firmly set and tightly sealed if they are to stay in place. Operable windows are made to move, and that's what they tend to do in high winds. Fixed windows are a better solution.

Sometimes a window's intended purpose makes fixed windows the best selection. An obvious example is a shop window, which is meant to attract interest in what's inside the store. Displays, price banners, or enticing views into a store are impeded with the extra hardware needed for operable windows. Moreover, security considerations make fixed (and burglar-alarmed) windows the preferable selection. Security might also mean fixing a window so people, particularly children, are safe from falling out of otherwise accessible window openings.

So, even though it's nice to open a window every once in a while, there are a lot of very good reasons why those who build a building might want to take that option away by having windows that simply don't open.

WHAT GOES ON BETWEEN THE CEILING AND THE FLOOR?

One suspects that when songwriter Paul Simon said, "One man's ceiling is another man's floor," he was talking about apartment buildings, where this concept basically is true. Two stories stacked one on top of the other share a common structure divided only by a layer of plaster or gypsum board on the lower story's ceiling, and perhaps a wood deck and floor for the story above. For multistory commercial buildings, the concept is more complex.

The floor-to-ceiling height (that is, the usable room height) of most contemporary office buildings measures 8 feet. Yet the height measured from story to story can be 10 or 12 feet, or more, because above the ceiling of one story and beneath the floor of the story above it is an extra 2 or 3 feet. Mechanical ducts, electric wiring, and pipes for water are hidden in this space above the ceiling, usually attached to the structure of the floor above with metal straps. The ceiling itself is suspended from this structure by metal wires, hence the name *suspended ceiling*. The tiles in the ceiling can be popped out of their frames to allow workers easy access to all the ducts and doodads above. (As an aside, those tiny holes that are punched into ceiling tiles are there to help absorb the noise in the room, whereas a solid-surface ceiling tile would just reflect the sound back into the space.)

In recent years manufacturers have developed a series of products that work as a mechanical space on the floor, rather than above the ceiling. The floor surface that you walk on sits on top of metal pedestals that rest directly on the structural floor. Called *raised* or *access floors*, they allow access to services through the floor, which is usually covered with carpet tiles that are removable in strategic areas. Access floors are popular in building types that need a lot of electrical wiring, such as computer rooms.

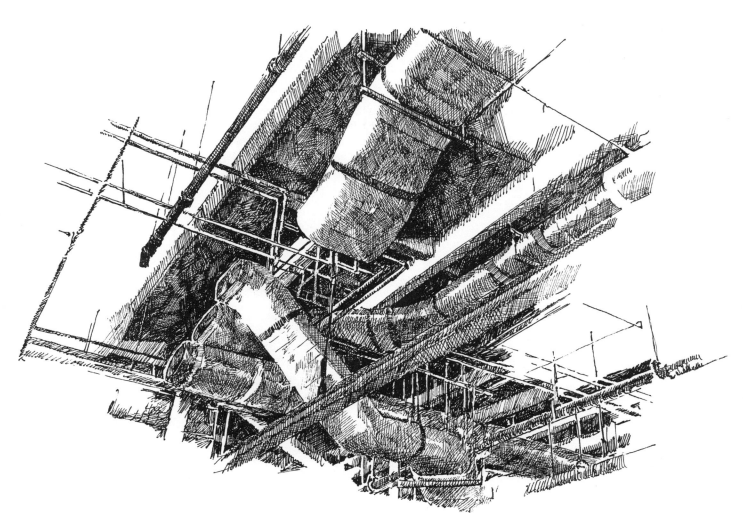

Service systems, including plumbing pipes, air ducts, electric wiring, and lighting systems are housed in the two or three feet between the ceiling and the floor.

Like most elements of architecture, choosing a lighting type depends on cost, efficiency, appropriateness, and beauty. Incandescent lamps, the regular old light bulbs of choice for most houses, were perfected by Thomas Edison in 1879. Edison used a carbon filament in an evacuated glass bulb

The Lever House, designed by Skidmore, Owings & Merrill, illuminates the New York City night sky with its fluorescent office lighting.

to create electric light. Today, the carbon filament had been replaced with tungsten, but the operating principle is the same—the filament is heated until it glows white-hot. The average incandescent bulb today burns for approximately 2,000 hours, compared to Edison's original 15-hour bulb. Incandescent lights give off a warm, orange-yellow light that is particularly flattering to human skin tones, which is probably the foremost reason for their popularity in places where people live. Standard light bulbs are also fairly cheap and can be used in all kinds of lamps. However, they are relatively inefficient, considering the amount of energy it takes to run them compared with the amount of light they give off. In addition, as much as 80 percent of the energy used to operate incandescents is dissipated in the form of heat, not a problem in most homes, but potentially uncomfortable given enough lamps in a large office space.

Fluorescent lamps, first marketed in 1934 and called "cold lights," require less energy to operate and are therefore an economic boon to owners of large buildings with lots of light fixtures. The typical fluorescent lamp is a cylindrical glass tube sealed at both ends, which contains a mixture of inert gas. At the end of the tube is a cathode that supplies a beam of energy to excite the electrons in the inert gas, which makes them give off photons—light. A fluorescent lamp must be hooked up to a ballast (a controller) that supplies sufficient electricity to start the lamp operating. The steady electron discharge produces ultraviolet light, which is absorbed by a phosphor coating on the inside of the glass tube and is reradiated as visible light.

Standard fluorescents produce a bluish-white "cool" light, which can actually cause colors to appear truer (if not as flattering to humans) than the warm tones of incandescent light. There is an increasingly wide range of "whites" available in fluorescents—the ones with more reds and blues give a truer color rendition, but take more energy to operate for the amount of light they give off.

By the way, the yellowish lamps found in parking lots and on highways (the ones that can render a peaches-and-cream complexion into a bilious Frankenstein pallor) are called low-pressure sodium lamps. Despite their ghastly color rendition, they operate at a very high ratio of light given off to power needed, making them very economical for outdoor use.

Regardless of lamp type, in architectural parlance a *lamp* is an artificial source of light, such as a bulb or a fluorescent tube; a *luminaire*, or lamp fixture, is a complete lighting unit, including the lamp, the lamp housing, and all the parts needed to connect to the power supply; and *light* is the radiant energy that produces a visual sensation. Now that you know this, you must say, "Turn out the lamps," "Oh, what an attractive table luminaire," and "I see the light."

How do elevators work?

You don't quite trust them, do you, especially the fancy glass ones that look as though they are held up with spider webs. Nevertheless, elevator technology is rather simple. Although there are many variations, there are still only two basic types of elevators: hydraulic and electric.

Hydraulic elevators use a piston to raise and lower the elevator car. The piston is located in a fluid-filled cylinder. By adjusting the pressure on the fluid, you can push the piston (and, in turn, the elevator car) up and

Elevators for buildings over six stories tall are always electrically generated.

down. The piston requires a well dug beneath the elevator pit. The length of piston required and the slow speed at which a hydraulic elevator operates limit its height range to 60 feet (a five- or six-story building).

By contrast, electric elevators are limited in height only by building technology (see pp. 169–170). They operate by means of wire ropes that are pulled over an electric hoisting machine (that looks like a giant pulley) and are attached to counterweights. These are the kind of elevators made famous in adventure movies when the bad guy cuts the rope and the good (but hapless) guy goes crashing to the ground. In real life, this can't happen. All elevator frames are equipped with stops, which are either *car safeties* or *counterweight safeties* that slow down, stop, and hold the car should the wire cables break or slip their fastenings.

Choosing the right system of elevators for a high-rise building can be a design problem unto itself, and many architects will hire an elevator specialist for a particularly complex job. The designer must take into account the location and size of the elevators (they must be large enough to accommodate wheelchairs and special equipment, such as hospital stretchers, in some instances); location and size of the machine room; how many people will be using the elevators (and therefore how many elevators), travel speed, and patterns of use (for example, in an office building the heaviest use of the elevator might be from 8:30 to 9:00 A.M.); lobby size; fire and safety requirements; barrier-free requirements; and control and calling systems.

As buildings get taller, elevator systems get more complicated. For example, both 110-story twin towers of the World Trade Center have "sky lobbies" at the forty-fourth and seventy-eighth floors. In terms of elevators, this means the tower acts like three buildings stacked on top of one another. The passenger can ride an elevator to the forty-fourth floor, catch a second to the seventy-eighth floor, and then ride a third, high-speed express to the top floor. An alternate route is the express elevator from the ground to the seventy-eighth floor, then up and away to the top. With greater building height also has come greater elevator speed. For decades New York's Empire State Building elevators held the record with 1,200 feet per minute; today, Chicago's John Hancock elevators ascend at 1,800 feet per minute.

Who was a founder of the modern movement?

"God is in the details" and "Less is more" are the watchword phrases attributed to Ludwig Mies van der Rohe (1886–1969), one of the founders of the modern movement, and one of the leading teachers of the Bauhaus (see pp. 124–125). They refer, respectively, to the modernist concepts of fine craftsmanship in every aspect of the design and the minimalist appearance so new at the time and so familiar to us today. While "glass boxes" now are denigrated as stark and boring, Mies's buildings stand out as gems, copied ad nauseum but unmatched in elegant simplicity.

Mies was as good as his words. A leading architect in Germany during the 1920s, he emigrated to the United States in 1937, where he took over the architecture department at Illinois Institute of Design (known at that time as the Armour Institute). During his extremely influential tenure, he designed many of the new buildings on the campus, as well as the campus master plan. Perhaps most famous is the one-story Crown Hall (1956), known for the "godliness" of its structural and connection details.

Mies also was architect of New York's Seagram Building, today a classic example of the modern movement and a well-known city landmark. The thirty-eight-story structure, completed in 1958 counts bronze-tinted glass and exposed bronze-covered columns among its elegant details.

Ludwig Mies van der Rohe was a master of detail of the modern movement, as illustrated by the elegant Barcelona Pavilion, built in 1929 for the International Exposition in Barcelona, Spain.

WHO WAS CHARLES-EDOUARD JENNERET?

A house is a machine for living was said by the prolific Le Corbusier (Charles-Edouard Jenneret, 1887–1965), who, as author of forty books and many more pamphlets and articles, said a lot of things.

Corbu's career as an artist and his equally prolific architectural career speak louder than his words. His concept of the house as a machine for living speaks of the modernist fascination with machines and industrialization as the pathway to a better life for the masses. Corbu's housing design style of his earlier career is clearly expressed in the Villa Stein (at Garches) and the Villa Savoie (at Poissy), both built in the late 1920s. These villas symbolized the rules that Le Corbusier thought were necessary for the new, healthful residential architecture that was to be brought about: free-standing columns at the ground level, glass walls, continuous strip windows, flat roofs (often topped by gardens), and open interior plans. With their white walls and open, light-filled interiors, Corbu's villas are often compared (in a positive way) with health sanitoriums.

The Pavilion Suisse, a university dormitory in Paris (1932) and the City of Refuge for the Salvation Army in Paris (1931) are much larger buildings that reflect Le Corbusier's ideas about machines for living on a larger scale. Also concerned with an even broader scale, he planned the Capitol Complex of Chandigarh, India (1950s) including many of its major buildings, and conceived the Plan for a City of Three Million Inhabitants that was (some might say, mercifully) never built.

Corbu evolved a multifaceted style through his long career, working on many other building types, including the Cathedral at Ronchamps (1955) and the monastery at La Tourette (1960). His only work in the United States is the Carpenter Center for the Visual Arts (1963) on the campus of Harvard University.

How did he get to be Corbu when he was born Charles Edouard Jenneret? He intentionally brought it on himself—by adopting his maternal grandfather's last name, Le Corbusier, as an architectural pseudonym. Some biographers claim that this extra name let him give himself an extra persona—that of the creative genius-inventer. Le Corbu, which means "the crow," quickly followed. This is easy to understand if you have ever seen a photo of him in his signature spectacles with their round, heavy black frames.

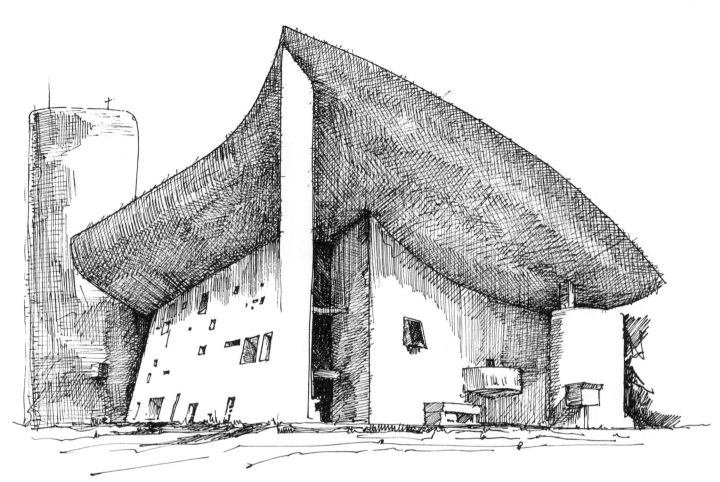

Le Corbusier, who believed "a house is a machine for living," illustrated a more romantic vision for the chapel of Notre Dame du Haut at Ronchamps, France, completed in 1955.

CHAPTER THREE ARCHITECTS AND THEIR PRACTICE

Architect joke:
Archie: How many architects does it take to screw in a light bulb?
Tex: You just can't tell—every project is different.

Every architectural project *is* different. Even if an architect were to take a single set of plans, and have the same construction team build them, the site would be different. That means the orientations to surrounding buildings, the prevailing winds, and the sun would be different, so the buildings would perform differently. And the subground conditions which affect the way a structure is designed and built, wouldn't be the same. And, of course, such a hypothetical situation is generous to begin with. Typically, it is only with prefabricated, modular buildings that the same design documents get used more than once.

It is the individuality of each building project that turns the craft and science of building design into the art of architecture. There are important distinctions among the art, the craft, and the science of architecture. The science is theory. Craft is application of that theory. Art is creative mastery of the craft. Force equals weight times distance is a scientific principle that is applied to the craft of successfully cantilevering a concrete slab. Fallingwater, one of Frank Lloyd Wright's most famous houses, is the artful use of the cantilever form in concrete and stone.

So what makes a great architect? Who is this Frank Lloyd Wright, and why does everyone talk about him? Did you know that the architect of the Declaration of Independence, Thomas Jefferson, was also the architect of his own house, Monticello, and of the University of Virginia central campus?

What is architectural style, and how does such a thing come to be? And what peculiarities of the creative process do architects work within? Isn't it odd, for instance, that architecture is the mastery of three-dimensional space, yet architects communicate with one another, with engineers, and with builders through drawings, a two-dimensional medium? And, finally, who is looking over the architect's shoulder to guarantee that buildings don't fall down or threaten their occupants unreasonably (and how do architects keep those guidelines from becoming restraints)?

Let's step into the world of architects and their practice and find out.

WHAT IS "FIRMNESS, COMMODITY, AND DELIGHT"?

It is the architect's version of faith, hope, and charity; the basic tenets of what every building should possess. First coined by Vitruvius, the Roman architect and military engineer who served Julius Caesar and Caesar Augustus, the phrase was part of his definition of the role of the architect, whom Vitruvius saw as a widely and liberally educated individual. As opposed to a more narrowly visioned master builder, Vitruvius said that the architect was a technically skilled and sensitive man (of course, they were all men at the time) who was capable of imbuing a building with *firmitas* (propriety), *utilitas* (convenience), and *venustas* (beauty).

The Temple of Fortuna Virilis in Rome was built 100 years after Vitruvius proclaimed that architecture must have "firmness, commodity, and delight."

This definition has survived 2,000 years as a part of Vitruvius's *Ten Books of Architecture*, the only books from antiquity on the practice of architecture. The books presented a wide variety of topics, including town planning, construction of war machines, astronomy, and how to prepare concrete. Perhaps best known is Book III, which contains chapters describing the Ionic, Corinthian, and Doric orders, the first systematic description of the classical language of architecture.

Vitruvius would have been sympathetic to the writing of the book you are holding in your hands; his tomes contained many sketches, and he strove to define in clear terms the professional building jargon of his day. His popularity in the profession and his work are continually revived and brought to the forefront by architects and architecture writers alike. Through many copyings and translations his three watchwords have become the catch phrase, "firmness, commodity, and delight."

Perhaps a modern translation would be "structures, appropriateness, and aesthetics." A building first of all has to be structurally sound, keep out the elements, and keep its occupants comfortable. Second, it must be fitting to the use for which it is intended—a school must be a place conducive to learning, a church must invoke feelings of worship, and a house must be able to serve as a home. Third, the building must be pleasing to the senses—sight, touch, hearing, and even smell—otherwise, it's just construction and not architecture.

What is the difference between an architect and an engineer?

Most architects will tell you "salary." Then there are those who say the only difference between them and engineers is that architects have a sense of creativity and aesthetics. Engineers usually say that not only do they have their feet on the ground, but they know where the ground is. Suffice it to say that many engineers are in clouds most of us couldn't imagine and many architects have their feet firmly on the ground, including construction-site mud. And, of course, vice versa.

There are structural differences between them, however. School is where it begins. For one thing, a different kind of person wants to go to architecture school than to engineering school because there are different public perceptions of the two professions. Engineering is eggheaded and architecture is artsy. Students of both professions spend their first two years studying the basic arts and sciences courses, often sharing the same classes in structures, calculus, biology, physics, chemistry, drafting, English literature, history, psychology, and so on. The emphasis in engineering school is on lessons of logic, stacked one on top of the other. Architecture schools stress visual analysis, synthesis, and overall creativity. Again, this is a gross overgeneralization.

In their third years, architecture and engineering curricula take very different directions. Architecture students continue in the direction of the art and science of design in general, while construction-related engineering students concentrate on the science of particular aspects of design. Engineering students specialize in such subjects as civil, electrical, mechanical, and structural engineering. Architecture students generally generalize (and, depending on the school, they may complete a five-year curriculum to obtain a professional degree or obtain a master's degree in architecture following a bachelor's degree in architecture or another discipline).

Once graduated, engineers are considered trained entry-level specialists. They can often take their professional examination within a year, and get paid on average about 150 percent of what beginning architects earn. In addition, architects must serve an internship, often of three years or more, before being allowed to sit for their professional examination. At that point, career paths are so varied that there are few true general truths left. One is that architects tend to stick to the building sciences and they typically are generalists (they know nothing about everything, a wag might say), while engineers work in many applications, construction related and otherwise, and tend to be specialists (they know everything about nothing, our wag counters).

"Architects know nothing about everything while engineers know everything about nothing." The beauty of engineering comes from elegant solutions, as evidenced in this cable suspension bridge.

If a building fell down during the reign of Hammurabi, in Babylon around 2000 B.C., and killed somebody, the law called for the architect to be put to death. The penalties are different these days, but the professional responsibility is no less crucial.

The architect's responsibility doesn't require that a building function particularly well—even professionals are allowed to be imperfect (for instance, no lawyer will guarantee that you will win a lawsuit, just that you will get competent representation). "Standard of care" is a phrase used to express professional responsibility. Generally speaking, the performance of any architect is judged against what a reasonably prudent architect at the same time and place would do under the same circumstances. In court, this is often determined through the testimony of experienced architects who serve as expert witnesses.

One area in which architects do have a constant obligation is the life and safety of anyone using or even passing by a building. One reason for this is that architects tend to have a deep sense of humanity, but one cannot discount the fact that many architects find themselves named in lawsuits for alleged errors or omissions that most people would find very difficult to foresee.

A fairly well-known example involved the Hancock building in Boston, designed by I. M. Pei & Partners. The building is a tower of mirror glass. In January 1973, while the building was still under construction, a windstorm cracked and broke dozens of the double-glazed windows. Eventually, all the glass on the building had to be replaced. The public perception was that the glass wasn't fastened well enough to the metal window frames, which implicated the architect's design. The cracking and breaking was really caused by an insufficient understanding of the behavior of coated glass, a fairly new high-rise construction material at the time.

High-rise double glazing with uncoated glass had proven itself over time. The two sheets of glass are soldered directly to a strip of lead between them (called a spacer), which holds the glass in place and keeps water out even though wind and air-pressure changes jiggle the glass back and forth ever so slightly thousands of times a day. (As anyone knows who has broken a piece of wire by bending it repeatedly, this back-and-forth action—called *cycling*—creates significant destructive stress.)

The problem with the Hancock glazing was that the outside sheets of glass were coated with a reflective material that contains chrome. When soldered to the spacer, the coating did something nobody expected. It bonded the solder molecularly to the glass. The bond was so strong that as the glass cycled back and forth, it started microscopic cracks in the relatively weak lead spacer. As those cracks grew over time, they moved directly into the glass. The cracks in the glass eventually grew enough to be seen, and worse, to weaken the glass enough to allow it to break and fall off the building. That is all logical enough, but it's the kind of unforeseeable thing that unfortunately must come to light only through experience. The architect's design in that instance was not found to be faulty, by the way.

I. M. Pei & Partners demonstrated professional responsibility and ethical behavior in solving the problem of glass that wouldn't stay in place on the John Hancock Building in Boston.

WHY DO SOME ARCHITECTS HAVE "AIA" AFTER THEIR NAMES?

"AIA" stands for the American Institute of Architects, which, with about 55,000 members, is the largest professional association of architects in the United States. It is the architects' equivalent of the American Bar Association for lawyers, and the American Medical Association for doctors.

An architect must have a license to practice in order to become a full member of AIA. Licenses are issued by each individual state, after successful completion of an examination that qualifies the architect as proficient in the skills necessary to protect the health, safety, and welfare of the public.

Members of the American Institute of Architects are supported by staff at the AIA's Washington, D.C. headquarters, located behind the historic Octagon House.

The AIA was founded in 1857 as a regional society in New York City. In 1889 the organization expanded nationwide, and its membership totaled 465 men. The AIA headquarters is now located in Washington, D.C., in a modern office building that carefully surrounds the historic Octagon House. The AIA provides a number of services to its membership, including awards programs; continuing education programs; a number of special interest committees; an annual conference; the AIA Press, which publishes a number of special interest books; lobbying on Capitol Hill; and a monthly newsletter and a magazine. The AIA also provides community design assistance and sponsors a "search for shelter" program for the homeless.

In addition to the national headquarters, the AIA has 301 regional, state, and local chapters that both cater to the special needs of local architects and serve as a communications link to the national headquarters. The local chapter is a good place to start if you are looking for an architect, or have specific questions about architecture.

WHY DO ARCHITECTS' DRAWINGS LOOK WEIRD?

When your architect sketches or renders a perspective drawing for your prospective building, it doesn't look weird at all, because the perspective is a "real-life" drawing that portrays how the building would actually look to the human eye. These drawings, often called *presentation drawings*, are designed to allow clients to understand how the building will look.

The other kinds of drawings that the architect prepares may look weird to the layperson, because they are intended to fulfill other purposes, such as helping the architect to expand design ideas and telling the contractors and builders how to put the building together. The three basic kinds of working drawings are elevations, plans, and sections.

Elevations show the facades of the buildings as if they were perfectly flat. Because elevations do not adjust for perspective as the human eye does, they may look weird and out of proportion. The building materials on such drawings are represented by conventional symbols; for example, bricks are often drawn as straight horizontal lines. Elevations show all the building components and materials on the building face drawn to scale, which means all the actual dimensions of the components are in their exact relative proportions on the drawing. For instance, a common scale for architectural drawings is ⅛ of an inch (on the drawing) equals one foot (on the building itself). The architect would call this an "eighth-scale" drawing. If the eighth-scale drawing of the facade measures 6 inches wide, the actual building facade is 48 feet wide. If the drawing shows windows that measure ¾ inch tall, the windows on the building will be 6 feet tall.

Plans and sections also show building components and materials drawn to scale, and use a series of symbols to indicate specific materials. *Plan* usually connotes a *floor plan*, meaning that the drawing shows the view looking straight down at the floor, usually from a height of 4 feet above the floor. Everything you see on the drawing is as if a cut had been made horizontally across the building at this 4-foot height. Elements that are cut through, such as walls, are often indicated by blacked-in lines. If architects wish to indicate that there is something special above the 4-foot line that wouldn't be seen by looking down, for instance, a skylight, they draw that element on the plan with a dashed or dotted line. Architects also draw *ceiling plans*, showing everything you would see if you looked up, but these are less common.

Section drawings work the same way as plans, except that they show a vertical cut through the building. It's as if the outside wall of the building were missing and the insides of the building were exposed straight on to the viewer. Sections can be drawn at any point in the building; usually the architect "takes a section" where it will give the most information about

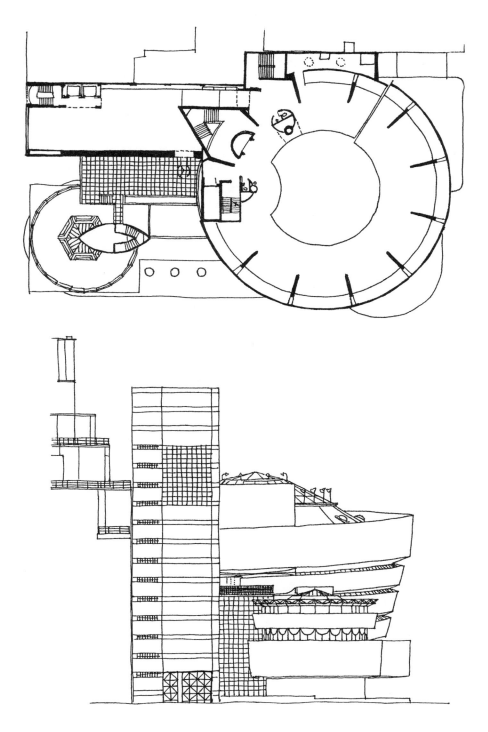

Frank Lloyd Wright's drawing of the Guggenheim Museum in New York is drawn to exact scale measurements.

how the building works. Elements that are cut through, such as the floors, are often shown with blacked-in lines.

Plans, sections, and elevations go through many iterations at the architect's hand. The early iterations, called *schematics,* are used by the architect and client to develop ideas. The refined ideas become *working drawings* that are used by the contractor and workers to build the project. Often, construction of particular elements of the building needs more detailed instruction, and the architect will prepare more elaborate drawings of these elements, appropriately called *detailed drawings* or *details.*

In addition to being drawn without perspective correction, and pressing into service material symbols and conventions, architects' drawings look weird because, more often than not, they're blue! Blueprints are architects' accepted means of creating multiple copies of the large sheets of drawings that must reach many sets of hands in order for the building to get built.

Strictly speaking, our *blueprints* of today are misnomered. The term *blueprint* refers to a photographic copying process developed in the 1830s by Sir John Herschel in England. Herschel discovered a compound that, when exposed to light, turned treated drawing paper blue when a copy was processed. The parts of the paper covered with ink lines stayed white during the process. Therefore, original blueprints were white line drawings on blue paper. Today, what we call blueprints—white paper with blue line drawings—actually are the result of an ammonia-based dying process for copying. (And, they may be black instead of blue.)

The blueprint process developed a century and a half ago was a revolutionary boon for architects, who no longer needed to trace over and over sets of drawings. In the past decade, the use of computers for drawings is just as revolutionary in its own way. Drawings stored in a computer memory can easily be retrieved and printed out on a printer many times over. More important, creating drawings on computer (called *computer-aided design and drafting,* or CADD) has revolutionized the way architects prepare drawings, and even the way that they think about design (see pp. 166–168).

WHAT IS A BUILDING CODE?

A building code is the *law* defining the parameters that a building must meet before it can be built. When an architect prepares a building design, the local building official must check that the design complies with the requirements of the code. If the building meets code, the architect receives a building permit and construction may get underway. During construction and after the building is completed, the official will check again to make sure that the actual construction complies with the building code. If it does, the building gets a certificate of occupancy, allowing users to occupy the building. If it doesn't, the construction must be adjusted, and the building reinspected until the official is satisfied. It is much the same process as getting your car inspected for state vehicular registration.

The shape and form of individual buildings, and therefore of cityscapes like those of New York, are determined in large measure by building codes.

In all fairness, that description simplifies a very complicated process. Large commercial buildings need to meet many kinds of code compliance: Fire and life safety, handicapped accessibility, structural, mechanical, electrical, plumbing, interior finishes, and elevators all may be governed by separate codes in any given jurisdiction. A building code itself weighs in with about 800 pages of text, and every year about 400 changes are proposed to its wording. Different types of buildings, classified by how the building is being used and by the structural type of the building, must meet different code requirements. Is it any wonder that most large architecture offices have code specialists, or hire outside consultants to check their designs for code compliance?

Building codes in this country are one of the last holdouts of Jeffersonian democracy—their enforcement is relegated to the smallest governmental group that is willing to adopt its own code. Consequently, there now are 3,900 building codes in effect at village, town, city, county, and state levels. The code of the smallest jurisdiction normally takes precedence, unless the building project is being funded by a larger jurisdiction (for example, a state office building in a small town most likely will have to adhere to the state code). This gets really confusing if the codes have different requirements—and there is good likelihood that they will. The architect has to know which code is in effect on the building's site.

There is one bright note—most of the building codes at all jurisdictions in the country have been adapted from just three *model codes*, which lay out basic life safety and structural requirements. (The model building codes have no force of law unless adopted by a jurisdiction.) Use of these three codes is regionally oriented: One is popular in the Northeast and Midwest, another in the South, and the third on the West Coast. Each of the model codes responds to regional concerns, for example, the western code has more stringent requirements for earthquake design. A local jurisdiction may adopt the model code as is, or make further adjustments (called *adapting* or *amending*) so that the code is more responsive to its local needs. While the model codes are updated every year, a local jurisdiction may update its code as often as it chooses, which means that the architect not only has to find the proper code, but also the properly dated version of that code in effect. It is no surprise that many architects are in favor of one federal building code, locally enforced.

WHO OVERSEES CONSTRUCTION?

This is a question that has been at the root of construction-industry liability for generations. And for good reason. Even when a building succumbs to the forces of nature, as in a severe earthquake, it is the nature of people to want to place blame, especially if it is a matter of personal injury or worse. We decide through the judicial system that one or more parties are at fault. In the case of an earthquake, maybe the owner is blamed for skimping on the construction budget, the designer is blamed for not anticipating the stress of the quake on the building, or the contractor is blamed for poor construction technique. Then every one of them is suddenly thrown into an atmosphere of excuse making, fact finding, and finger pointing. It gets to the point where one would think nobody was to blame for a building failure. But that's the opposite of the truth. Each person on a project design and construction team shares in the responsibility of that building's subsequent performance, all in different ways.

The person most in charge on the construction site is the general contractor. Typically, the owner contracts with an architect, who prepares the blueprints and other documents necessary for construction and assists the owner in hiring a contractor on the basis of lowest cost for completing the project, experience in the project type and area conditions, financial stability, and other stipulations important to the owner. Usually, the selection process involves the owner publicizing, often through industry periodicals, that a project is open for bidding. Interested general contractors calculate, from the construction documents prepared by architects and engineers, how much it would cost them to build the proposed project. The owner chooses from those *open* bids.

A *closed* bidding process means that only selected contractors have been invited to submit bids. Closed bidding is usually required for complex private construction jobs. Because of the potential for inside deals and other abuses, laws require almost all government construction work to be let to open bidding.

The architect does not enter into a contract with the contractor in normal circumstances. The architect's job is to design a building and look out for the owner's benefit in every service the architect has contracted to perform. The architect's obligation to work in the best interest of the client is generally referred to as the architect's *fiduciary responsibility*.

The contractor, on the other hand, is obligated to build what is requested, but is allowed to look out for his or her own interests. That means the contractor looks very hard at the project cost, both for the sake of profitability and to uphold his or her reputation for bringing jobs in on time and within budget. To be able to bring the bid to reality, the contractor has to be in charge of the construction site. Although there aren't any laws that say so explicitly for all cases, it is generally accepted (because of

On the construction site, the general contractor reigns as king, but the architect often looks out for the owner's interest.

the history of how courts have been deciding such questions) that the contractor dictates *means and methods* of construction. As far as liability goes, that means the contractor is responsible if something gets built differently from the way it was designed, if something gets damaged during construction, or if somebody gets hurt on the construction site.

Since the architect is often responsible for making sure the contractor is doing the work the owner wanted done, it would make sense for the architect to have someone competent on the job site at all times to make sure that the contractor doesn't cut corners to the detriment of building quality. For a number of reasons, however, this is not at all practical. For one, the cost to the architect of having a full-time employee dedicated to a job site for a year or more is enormous. And few owners are willing to pick up that salary as a reasonable reimbursable expense without a lot more direct control over the construction supervisor.

Beyond economics, though, architect supervision of contractor performance doesn't work because of the cult of personality on the job site. Few contractors enjoy, or even want, someone to be looking over their shoulders. Because the job eats up potential billable hours, architects are known to send junior architects to perform site observation. No experienced contractor is going to take well to the advice of someone with limited construction experience.

In some cases, the owner hires someone separate from the architect or contractor whose sole responsibility is to manage construction. The best construction managers typically are highly experienced architects, engineers, or former contractors who know job sites as well as the project contractor, which is necessary because their job is to oversee the contractor's work. Many large corporations even have in-house construction management divisions because they've found that close supervision of the whole process of design and construction can save a lot of money. For a developer (who builds as a financial speculation that the building can be leased or sold for a profit to an end-user), saving during construction is the chief concern. But even at millions of dollars, construction costs are a relatively minor expense for a competitive corporation building its own facilities and thinking of long-term costs. Operational expenses over decades of building use can be reduced significantly if the building is put together and works the way it should. So developer/owner profitability, both short-term and long-term, is the chief rationale behind hiring a construction manager.

There is another cadre of people responsible for what goes on during construction. Government inspectors, of one sort or another, have to check the legality of design plans and resulting construction—from houses to nuclear power plants—in virtually every legal jurisdiction in the United States. The laws they enforce are building codes and other statutes that protect the life safety of building users and the population at large. Exits have to be accessible in case of fire, and big enough or numerous enough to let everyone out quickly, for example. Fireplaces and chimneys have to be built a certain way. And certain construction techniques have to be employed in areas that have a high probability of earthquakes, floods, storms, heavy snow, or some other condition naturally stressful on buildings. Building officials also oversee safety on the construction site. In fact, the problem is so important to the public that there is a federal agency, the Office of Safety and Health Administration (OSHA), responsible for construction safety.

Although at first glance it may seem that a construction site is going to be filled with more overseers at odds with one another than subcontractors actually doing the labor, that isn't so. Well, maybe sometimes it is, but not until a project is in real trouble—financial, legal, or otherwise. Usually all the design and construction team members know one another, what is expected of each, and how well each individual performs. If they have teamwork, all parties leave the job happy and the building will likely be a good one. In the final analysis, quality construction isn't a matter of defining who is responsible for what, it is more a matter of getting people onto the job who want to do responsible work in a collective effort.

How is dirt kept from caving in on a construction site?

Dirt is deadly stuff. Unfortunately, because it looks nice and solid when you're standing on it, too many people get careless when digging and get crushed or smothered when the sides of a hole they're in collapse. The potential for damage increases with the size of the hole. In the case of a very large excavation (digging the foundation for a large building, for example), a collapse could affect the stability of surrounding streets and buildings. That is why you'll notice, whenever you see a building foundation being dug, that the first bit of construction on the site is excavation bracing.

There are two basic strategies for keeping dirt from sliding into a hole. One is to slope the sides. Federal regulation for construction-worker safety requires that any excavation going deeper than 5 feet have sides sloped at 45 degrees, or be braced. Bracing is more expensive and complicated than sloping the sides. But in cases where the excavation must be deep, or the building site is restricted, bracing is the only practical choice.

A moderate-size building, say 100 feet on a side, requires a foundation hole of 110 feet on a side if the foundation is 5 feet deep and has sloped sides. That doesn't sound too unreasonable. But a building of that size is likely to have at least two basement floors, which would require a 30-foot-deep foundation and sides of 160 feet. Not only does that require a lot of land for the construction site, it is an incredible amount of extra excavation and infill.

The alternative is to dig the sides of a hole straight up and down, build a wall to hold up the dirt, and brace the wall to resist the force of earth and groundwater pushing in on the hole. Because the wall has to hold back the earth as excavation goes on, the wall structure must be in place before digging even begins. It may sound impossible to you to build a wall underground, but that is exactly what is done. There are three common means of building underground wall structures. The method chosen depends on soil conditions, common local practice, extent of the excavation, and site accessibility. As always, cost is a factor as well.

The strategy for firm clay soil, free of obstructions and above the water table, starts with workers driving I-beams into the ground. They crane-lift each I-beam pile into position and cap it with a piston-driven pile driver. The banging noise is jarring, but if all goes well, a pile can be driven (like a big nail) 30 feet into the ground in less than 15 minutes. Once piles are driven every 6 to 10 feet all around the excavation site, workers proceed to dig them out. As they dig, they place heavy timbers, called "lagging" between the flanges of the freshly exposed I-beams. This is one case where a wall is built from the top down.

In looser soils, a common retaining-wall technique is to drive wood or steel sheet piles all the way around the soon-to-be excavated area to form a continuous subground barrier. Steel sheeting about a half an inch thick and vertically crimped to make it laterally stronger, is the standard material for a sheet pile retaining wall. To keep groundwater out of the excavation, standard sheet piles also have a flange running down one edge and a slot running down the other so side-by-side sheets slide together as each is hammered into the ground. Although more water resistant than the I-beams and lagging, sheet piles don't work well when excavation goes below the water table.

Where subground water is a problem, an engineer might have the contractor build a subground concrete wall. The construction crew members use a thin-bucketed digger with a long arm to carve a deep trench no more than a few feet wide, which they fill with steel reinforcement and concrete. The result, if all goes well, is a strong, watertight enclosure for a hole yet to be dug.

Temporary underground walls, called shoring, hold back soil from caving into an excavation site.

No matter what kind of retaining wall is used, there are two basic strategies for bracing it. One is to dig into the middle of the site, sloping the sides at 45 degrees until the center of the excavation is as far down as required. Steel struts are leaned against the sloped sides of the hole, braced against the ground at the bottom with the other end attached to the top of the retaining wall. (Typically, the struts are connected to horizontal I-beams—called "whalers"—attached along the top of the retaining wall.) The excavation crew then digs out the dirt beneath the struts and the hole is completed with minimal risk. Strut bracing is straightforward and fairly simple, but has the disadvantage of taking up a lot of space inside the foundation hole. They can be awkward to work around.

A strategy that allows a completely open foundation hole is to tie the retaining wall back into the soil behind it. If the surrounding ground conditions allow (including right-of-way from neighboring landholders), workers drill narrow holes into the sides of the excavation to create channels for subground anchors that extend downward and outward from the top of the retaining wall all around the excavation site. Workers put steel tendons into the anchor holes and pump grout to the bottom to hold the steel in place. Post-tensioning the anchored steel takes any slack out of the tendons. Once the steel is stretched, the rest of the hole is filled with dirt and the free end of the tendon is attached to a pile or whaler. The result is that the anchored and stretched tendons pull outward on the retaining wall much like tent guy wires, except that the tendons are buried underground.

Once the foundation is dug and braced, the hole is safe for construction workers. As the building goes up and fills the hole in the ground, bracing can be cut and removed (the building itself then holds the dirt back), it can be incorporated into the structure of the new building, or it might be left in place as useless underground junk waiting for years to surprise the next person who wants to build on the site.

WHO DECIDES HOW HIGH BUILDINGS IN A CITY SHOULD BE?

Building zoning ordinances are localized. In one town, the town council might decide whether a building is too tall, and might do so only if a citizen group made a formal petition against the building developer. In many cities, however, a governing body—be it a zoning board, a building commission, or a citizen's group—is recognized as the authority overseeing building height.

Ultimately, the government of, by, and for the people decides how high a building is in a city, but that only tells who, not why. The whys are many. In Washington, D.C., the U.S. Capitol building sets the unwritten height limit of any building in that city. So far, that restriction has held firm and is part of the reason the nation's capital maintains something akin to a small-town atmosphere.

Philadelphia had a similar informal height restriction: no building could be taller than the statue of William Penn atop the Philadelphia City Hall (548 feet). By 1970 only four buildings in Philadelphia were over thirty stories, and at the end of that decade, forty stories was about the top limit for the city's tallest towers. But in 1988, One Liberty Place, a sixty-one-story tower designed by Murphy/Jahn, and developed by Rouse & Associates, broke well above its low-lying surroundings and, at over 700

feet, surpassed the Penn statue. Whether that building serves as a landmark or merely a precursor to a high-rise takeover of the Philadelphia skyline remains to be seen. The current plan for Philadelphia calls for tall-building construction to be limited to the Market Street corridor.

Such aesthetic considerations aside, there are other, somewhat more practical, reasons for limiting the size of a building. For instance, the weight of a building on the ground that supports it is definitely a factor that architects consider. With some soils, typically deep clay or sandy ground, special means are necessary to keep buildings from sinking. That may take the form of piles sunk into the ground all the way through the soft soil to rock or solid ground or, where the soft soil is particularly thick, deep piles that don't rest on solid ground but resist the weight of the building through friction against the soil itself. Another method is to float the building on a large slab of concrete, which is only possible when the mass of a building is low with respect to its footprint (ground-floor area). In most cases, though, the weight of a building does not present a problem because the weight of even a large building is often less than the weight of the soil that was removed to form the building's foundation.

Regulatory authorities also take into account the effects on the neighborhood of a building's height. Tall buildings throw long shadows. They also tend to act like huge windscoops, sending fast-moving upper winds down to sidewalk level. And, as anyone knows who has walked the streets of Atlanta, they can be frightfully imposing when juxtaposed against low-rise surroundings.

In Washington, D.C., no structure may exceed the height of the Capitol building.

113

WHY DO ARCHITECTS PLACE STAIRWAYS SO FAR APART?

When you are walking through a large building, and decide to take the stairs instead of the elevator, it seems as though you have to walk to the ends of the earth (or at least to the ends of the building) to find them. Architects are not being sadistic as to where they place the stairways; they have your safety in mind. The paramount role that stairs play during a building fire emergency is the main reason.

Most residents of buildings with more than two stories have been cautioned that during a fire they should not attempt to use the elevators (which can easily fill with smoke, short out, or get trapped between floors) but rather should leave the building using the closest stairway. (In fact, many modern buildings have fire safety systems that automatically direct the elevator to the ground floor and lock them in place, so that only the firefighters can use them for rescue operations.) Almost every multiple-story building today, with the exception of houses, has two or more stairways, just in case the path to one should be blocked by fire. It makes sense to have stairways placed as far apart as possible, so that if one is blocked by fire, the other will be as far from the danger as possible.

There are limits to the distance allowed between stairways, however, which are based on years of studies and experience on how to evacuate people most safely from buildings. Governed by building codes, which vary in how these distances are calculated, the limit lies somewhere in the range of a person traveling no more than 150 feet in an unsprinklered building and 200 feet in a building with sprinklers in order to reach the exit (which in code parlance means the door to the stairways). In a long building with a lot of floor space, extra stairways have to be placed in the building to meet this code requirement.

Building fire stairs often have a closed-in fortresslike feeling. There is a good reason for that, too: Their special, heavy-duty construction permits them to hold up against fire and smoke for long periods of time, often longer than the rest of the building.

Every stair user has had the frustrating experience of entering a stairway on one floor of the building, and ascending or descending to the desired floor, only to find the door in the stairway locked. For security reasons, many building owners lock the doors leading from the stairway to the main part of the building. In that situation, never fear—the stairway door to the ground level *must* be unlocked, just in case there is a fire. Should you ever find one that is locked, report it to the authorities immediately—it is a code violation and a potentially life-threatening situation.

Stairs are placed far apart, usually at opposite ends of a building, to provide a better chance for building occupants to escape during a fire.

Why Are Some Stairs So Difficult to Climb?

"Because they are too steep!" most likely is your first answer, and you'd be right, partially right, anyhow. If you've ever walked up the stairs at Lincoln Center in New York, or climbed the pathway in Arlington Cemetery, you know firsthand that shallow stairs can be just as difficult to ascend (and descend) as a steep set. This is because comfort and safety of stair design depends on a combination of stair height (the *rise*) and stair tread width (the *run*). The rule of thumb for outdoor stair design says that

Spiraled stairs like these are only one of many kinds of stair designs that may be more or less easy to climb.

two times the height of the riser plus the length of the tread should equal 26 inches (as an example, a stair with a riser of 6 inches should have a tread of 26 − 12 = 14 inches.) Measure an uncomfortable stair sometime and see if it breaks this rule.

For stairs inside buildings other than residential units, most building codes today require that the stair tread width be a minimum of 11 inches, and the riser be a maximum of 7 inches high and a minimum of 4 inches high. This forms the basis of a good stair design (unless you've got size 12 feet, which are close to a foot long, and therefore longer than the tread width). Add proper railings, good lighting, and a nosing shape that can't catch the toe of your shoe and trip you, and you're halfway home. Other factors for good stair design are properly designed landings at the top and bottom of the staircase, a minimum of three stairs and a maximum of ten stairs in a single flight, and uniform riser height throughout, all to allow a walker's cadence to adjust to using the stairs.

The model building codes are currently in agreement about the 7-inch-maximum for risers and the 11-inch-minimum for treads (called the *seven-eleven* rule). This agreement was a long time coming, however, and many stairs were constructed before the rule became law, hence the number of weird stairs around. Also, the rule does not apply uniformly to residential units, and some of the most uncomfortable and dangerous stairs can be found in houses, where space is tight and steeper stairs with narrow treads are used to save room. A recent study on home safety, conducted by the Buffalo Organization for Social and Technical Innovation, reported that accidents on stairs result in 1.8 to 2.66 million disabling injuries per year. It is no wonder that many stair safety experts propose extending the seven-eleven rule to residential construction. Their opponents are skeptical about how much safer these stairs would be, and say it would cost too much in terms of the square footage it would take.

It should come as no surprise that the elderly, as a group, are particularly prone to stair accidents. According to the American Institute of Architects' report, "Design for Aging," a high percentage of the falls on stairs in elderly residences result from a single riser that has a height different from the uniform height of the rest of the risers. The report also calls for lighting the stairways, day and night, to a higher level than the surrounding lighting, and for stairways to be as short and straight as possible.

WHAT DOES IT MEAN WHEN A BUILDING HAS "FAILED," AND WHY DOES THAT HAPPEN?

Normally, when architects talk about a building that has failed, they are talking about a structural collapse that has rendered the building physically unusable. Structural failure results from a number of causes. A building, like any other commodity, will wear out if it is insufficiently maintained. Enough termites with no check on their nasty culinary habits can take out a wood frame building. Enough drops of water pelting steel, year after year, can cause enough rust to corrode the frame, collapse the structure, and presto! Failed building.

Failed buildings also result from insufficient design or construction. One of the most commonly cited examples involves the 1981 collapse of the suspended walkways in the Hyatt Regency Hotel in Kansas City, Missouri. The walkways were built with insufficient strength in the connections to support the weight of a crowd standing on them. When the structure collapsed, during a well-attended dance held in the hotel, the toll of 113 people killed and 186 injured made it one of the worst building disasters in modern history.

Pruitt-Igoe, St. Louis's great social experiment in architecture, "failed" in that it did not serve the people it housed.

Acts of God and nature also cause building failures, by putting more stress on buildings than they can withstand. In late 1989 alone, thousands of structures in the United States were destroyed by a major earthquake on the West Coast and Hurricane Hugo on the East Coast. Fires destroy structures without favoritism to coastal location. Although we are improving our track record tremendously in terms of construction practices and building codes, our structures are not yet completely disaster proof.

Buildings suffer other, more minor types of failures that do not render the building permanently unusable. These are referred to in the trade as failures of the building component, not the building itself, for example, a roof failure. (In fact, leaking roofs are the most common building component failure.) The more minor types of failure also have myriad causes, including insufficient design (a brick wall designed without weepholes or a way for water to drain may leak inside the building); insufficient construction (if the mason does not tie the two layers of a double brick wall together properly, the wall may tumble down); and insufficient materials (if the wrong type of mortar is used in the brick wall, it may crumble away and leave you with an untidy pile of bricks).

There is another type of building failure that occurs within a broad range of severity: *functional inacceptability*. Perhaps the most notorious example of functional inacceptability is the Pruitt-Igoe Housing project built in St. Louis in 1955. Designed with good intentions, the modern fourteen-story low-income housing blocks incorporated some of the best architectural theories of the time: clean lines and unornamented spaces; "streets in the air" corridors to give people a place to walk, talk, and congregate; and play spaces and laundry rooms (see pp. 124–125). Most of the inhabitants were poor blacks from the rural south who did not appreciate or want the finer points of modern, high-rise architecture. The buildings had a much higher vandalism rate than surrounding projects, crime was rampant in the "streets in the air." In short, the project did not work for the tenants, the tenants hated the project, and in 1972 Pruitt-Igoe was dynamited to the ground.

Pruitt-Igoe is the extreme example. But look around at the buildings you inhabit everyday. Functional misfits range from the minor inconvenience (you can't reach the towel rack from the tub) to the must-be-adjusted nuisance (did you turn off the fluorescent lights in your office and buy lamps because you couldn't stand the glare? Does the secretary wear two sweaters and keep an electric space heater under his or her desk?) to the outright failure (if the mechanical system is spewing out organisms that cause sick building syndrome, you better clear out, quickly) (see pp. 142–143). Part of the problem may be out-and-out poor design; another part of the problem is that buildings designed to accommodate a large number of people (that is, more than one) will not suit everyone perfectly all of the time.

WHO WAS OUR ONLY ARCHITECT PRESIDENT?

His name was Thomas Jefferson, and he served as our third president from 1801 to 1809. Perhaps the greatness of his statesmanship, coupled with his authorship of the Declaration of Independence, the Virginia Statute of Religious Freedom, and Notes on the State of Virginia, have caused his architecture to be recognized as a secondary profession.

In a poll taken by *Architecture* magazine in 1976 to mark the country's bicentennial, architects by a large measure most often nominated Jefferson's University of Virginia campus in Charlottesville as the "proudest achievement of American architecture." The two parallel rows of pavilions fronting the long sides of an exquisitely proportioned lawn form a perfect foil to the classical domed rotunda. The composition of brick buildings is linked by a classically proportioned colonnade.

Jefferson the architect probably is best known to the public as the designer of Monticello, his beloved hilltop house outside of Charlottesville. Many writers have called the domed, brick house "autobiographical," in

Architect President Thomas Jefferson designed his own home, Monticello, on a hilltop near Charlottesville, Virginia.

that it reflects Jefferson's democratic social ideals and political beliefs. One can also see the influence of Jefferson's fascination with the work of Palladio, the renowned sixteenth-century Italian architect who favored revival of the classical architecture of antiquity. Jefferson believed this monumental style of architecture was fitting for the great new republic he envisioned and created.

Monticello, which has been restored and is open to the public, also serves as a memorial to Jefferson's inventiveness (his many "gadgets," including his stereo-writing machine that automatically makes a copy of a handwritten document and his through-the-floor chronometer are on display) and his deep understanding of how to work with the land and climate (the hilltop location, well-placed windows, and underground wings all induce natural ventilation to help keep the house cool during the long, hot summers of Virginia.)

Jefferson also designed a new state capitol for Richmond and several houses around the Charlottesville area. His interest in architecture also extended into town planning. He prepared a plan for the extension of Richmond as well as studies for the new capital city of Washington, D.C., both of which were based on grids with alternating squares for buildings and open space.

WHO WAS FRANK LLOYD WRIGHT AND WHY DOES EVERYBODY TALK ABOUT HIM?

He is probably the greatest American architect who ever lived, and possibly one of the best architects ever. Wright, born in the Midwest in 1869, developed a true American architecture, suited to sweeping distances and

Frank Lloyd Wright's residential masterpiece, Fallingwater, built in 1935 at Bear Run, Pennsylvania, illustrates his unsurpassed ability to integrate site and architecture.

grown out of nature. During the first decade of the twentieth century, he designed many of his so-called prairie houses, with their long, horizontal lines and varied roof planes. The best known of the prairie houses are the Robie House in Chicago, built in 1908, and the Martin House in Buffalo, built in 1904. Wright is also renowned for his lifelong pioneer work with concrete, from the Chicago Unity Church (1906), to Fallingwater in Bear Run, Pennsylvania (1936), to the famous mushroom columns of the Johnson Wax headquarters in Racine, Wisconsin (1938), to the spiraling Guggenheim Museum in New York City (1959). During his long life, which ended in 1959 at the age of 89, Wright designed hundreds of buildings. A tally and description of the wonders of any of these works could fill volumes.

Wright's career began in 1887 as a draftsman apprenticeship in the office of Louis Sullivan (see pp. 46–47). Sullivan recognized Wright's talent early on, and within two years Wright was working as a designer. There are varying stories as to whether Wright quit or was fired from Sullivan's office (as well as varying stories as to the reason, most of which dally around Wright's moonlighting activities); nevertheless, Wright always referred to Sullivan as "Lieber Meister," and acknowledged Sullivan's work alone as having influenced his designs.

Wright also suffered personal tragedy throughout his life. In 1909 he fell in love with a client's wife (Mamah Cheney) and, refused a divorce by his wife Catherine, abandoned her and their six children to live in Europe with Mrs. Cheney. He eventually returned to the United States and settled at Taliesin (meaning "Shining Brow" in Welsh), the home he built for himself and his new family in Spring Green, Wisconsin. In 1914 a crazed servant went berserk, killed Mrs. Chaney and two of her children, and set a fire that destroyed most of the living portion of Taliesin. Wright was devastated, even more so by the yellow press's field day over his "just deserts," but he found the will to rebuild the house.

The following year brought Wright the commission to design the Imperial Hotel in Japan, and he remained in residence with an American sculptor named Miriam Noel for several years. After his return to the United States, Taliesin again caught fire, and once again Wright struggled financially to rebuild his beloved home. His wife finally granted him a divorce, and he married Noel, who had a history of mental instability and soon left him to live in California. She died there in a sanitarium soon after their divorce in 1924. Wright's third marriage to Olgivanna Lazovick, a divorcee from Montenegro, lasted until his death.

For good or bad, Wright was a colorful character—by most accounts a strikingly handsome man sharp of tongue and wit with a theatrical flair for flowing cravats and capes. Many found him irascible, egotistical, and totally overbearing. Luckily, enough clients recognized his genius sufficiently to tolerate (perhaps even enjoy) his personality.

What is the Bauhaus?

The Bauhaus was a twentieth-century school, a design philosophy, and a way of life. It was founded in Weimar, Germany, in 1919 by Walter Gropius and moved to Dessau in 1925. Many of the great architects of the century, including Mies van der Rohe (see pp. 86–87, 174), were associated with the Bauhaus. The school embraced design fields beyond architecture, and was open to craftsmen and artists of all types, including Joseph Albers and Paul Klee.

The Bauhaus Compound, established in 1925 in Dessau, served as stomping grounds for some of the century's greatest architects, including Mies van der Rohe and Walter Gropius.

The Bauhaus philosophy advocated that architecture be created for the workers, unity of art and technology, and team effort and collaboration in the design process. Post-World-War-I Germany was fertile ground for rebuilding, and the Bauhaus thought and way of life were in the right place at the right time. Many of the design legacies of this thinking—flat roofs and facades, expressed structure, and predominance of black and white with neutral-colored detailing—are still with us today.

The Bauhaus style caught on like wildfire in the United States, in large part because of an exhibition and accompanying catalog produced by New York's Museum of Modern Art in 1932. Its authors, historian Henry Russell Hitchcock and Philip Johnson, called the exhibit (which featured the work of Gropius, Le Corbusier, Mies, and J. J. Oud) the "international style," a label that stuck to the Bauhaus style of work thereafter. It is also known as "modern" architecture.

In the wake of the Nazis in Europe, many of the Bauhaus masters emigrated to the United States. Gropius arrived in 1937 to chair the department of architecture at Harvard; Mies reigned at the Illinois Institute of Technology. This style of building ruled (almost) absolutely supreme until the 1970s.

Now that we are in the "post-modern" era, it is chic to malign the "glass box" style of the modernists. To appreciate the elegance of the style, it is necessary to examine the work of the masters, because probably there has never been a style of design that looks and functions worse when it is copied poorly. Readers who wish to know more about how the Bauhaus developed should look at popular author Tom Wolfe's entertaining and disparaging *From Bauhaus to Our House*. Wolfe's book, which gives the flavor of the era, is most palatable with several grains of salt.

Why are great cathedrals not built anymore?

Actually, great cathedrals all over the world are being built, added to, and restored right now. But it is true that cathedrals today hold a very small part in most of our lives, especially compared with the Europe of 500 years or so ago when cathedrals were in their heyday.

Although cathedrals were first built in the fifth century—most notably St Paul's Outside the Walls in Rome, around 380 A.D., and Hagia Sophia in Constantinople (the city Turkish conquerers renamed Istanbul), around the year 530—the great Gothic masterpieces we most associate with the term "cathedral" weren't introduced until the thirteenth century. One of the first was Notre Dame in Paris, completed around 1250.

Structurally, cathedrals are wondrous. Using stone, a material whose strength is in compression, medieval builders created huge, high-ceilinged spaces unencumbered by columns and filled with the rich light of stained glass windows. Art and architecture became one as the craft of cathedral building pushed stonemasonry to the bounds of its creative and physical limits.

Wondrous as they still are (imagine how they must have awed the earth-

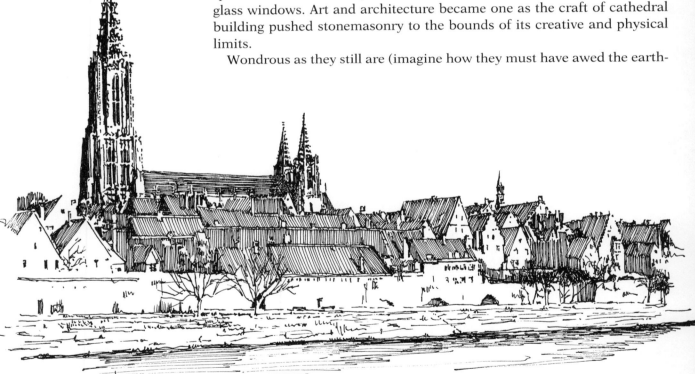

Great cathedrals, such as the Cathedral at Ulm in West Germany, were the order of the day for large cities in past centuries, they are rarities today. Two notable exceptions are the National Cathedral in Washington, D.C., completed in 1990, and St. John the Divine in New York City, which will not be finished until well into the next century.

bound folk of the Middle Ages), people today have become a bit jaded to large buildings that enclose huge, open, daylighted spaces. But before we try to blame John Portman (and the towering hotel atriums that have become his trademark) for the waning interest in cathedrals, we should look at some other factors.

It is hard to deny that European society has changed since 500 years ago. A cathedral is, by definition, the seat of a bishop. Of course that meant that cathedrals were, as they remain today, centers of religious authority. But beyond that, in the days when a cathedral overwhelmed the surrounding landscape by its sheer physical presence, it served also as landmark and civic center. On the cathedral grounds and in the building itself, townspeople gathered in major processional ceremonies for the great festivals of Christmas, Easter, Pentecost, and Corpus Christi. Furthermore, monastic cathedrals (those with a monastery) were, for all practical purposes, the sole centers of education until the Renaissance.

People living within the jurisdiction of a cathedral had a deep-seated personal interest in the edifice as well. The entire diocese contributed toward the building and maintenance of its cathedral, and the pride of achievement that drives most human endeavors was very much in evidence there. Masons (and, of course, their patrons) were always striving for the biggest and most dramatic naves, towers, and rose windows. Cathedrals may have taken several generations to complete, in some cases, but those who planned, built, and maintained them knew they would last tens of generations; maybe even hundreds. The civic pride that once inspired cathedral building currently is devoted more to convention centers or sports stadiums (whose standard life expectancy of twenty to fifty years actually may be a bit optimistic).

Now, with many cathedrals being pushed to the background of cityscapes as new buildings of concrete and steel jam in shoulder to shoulder, the modern outlook puts little value in a building type whose day of greatest glory has passed from human memory. It's expensive to build a cathedral, and it takes a long time. The National Cathedral in Washington, D.C. is just recently completed after over eighty-three years of construction. Monumental stone construction just isn't suited for the quick-turnaround building deals that most patrons of the building arts today demand.

But, in a way, cathedral building is progressing as it has since humans began building these great structures of stone around 1100 A.D. At St. John the Divine, in New York City, a few individuals are dedicating themselves to the nearly lost craft of stonecutting. Working under the tutelage of master masons, these aspiring stonecrafters, some of whom grew up in New York's slums, begin by learning how to shape blocks of sandstone roughly. Those further along in their learning might carve standard patterns or shapes, while intricate detail work falls to those who have achieved the higher levels of training and experience. With a slow and unsteady pace of upward growth of about a dozen feet a year, St. John the Divine isn't likely to be finished before the middle of the next century.

Why do buildings look different from one city to another?

Buildings look the way they do for two reasons. One, simply enough, has to do with function. The climate, terrain, and other natural and man-made forces and threats all have an effect on how a building looks. The log cabin chinked with mud and straw is a familiar backwoods style in North America because the building materials are handy, the construction is insulated from temperature extremes, and marauders—be they bears or relatives—can be locked out. The other reason buildings look as they do is style. Social, political, religious, commercial, and industrial influences all have an impact on the shape, mass, density, and decoration of our buildings.

In the United States, the major driving force in creating regional building style over the past few hundred years has been cross-cultural interaction. Native Americans had their own building styles—hogans, tipis, pueblos, and igloos among them—all developed under different environmental and social conditions. Large hogans allowed congregation and warmth for territorially established Native Americans in the Northeast and Northwest. Tipis provided shelter, allowed quick assembly and disassembly, and were transportable for nomadic Plains Native Americans. Pueblos used massive materials to hold the sun's heat and release it in the chill of evening hours, thereby moderating the severe temperature fluctua-

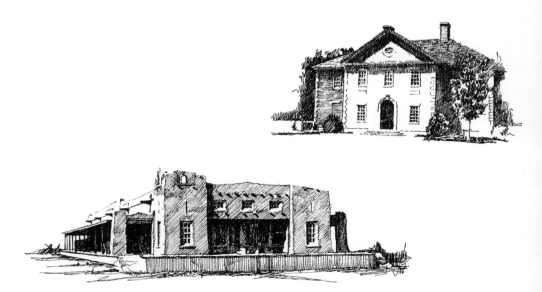

Historic precedents, perceived function, and response to climate and terrain give buildings a regional look.

tions of the southwestern desert. With abundant packed snow, Eskimos developed the low-lying, multi-compartmented igloo to resist the wind and cold of the Arctic regions.

When Europeans began to move into the New World, they brought their own solutions to creating shelter. In large part, the Dutch, English, and French colonized North America while the Spanish and Portuguese colonized South and Central Americas. In many areas, particularly the southern parts of North America, many cultures mingled—sometimes freely, sometimes with friction, but always with an architectural result that reflected the social and environmental situation of the region.

As it turned out, the French colonists—mostly explorers and trappers—had little influence on architectural style in colonial America, with notable exceptions, such as the Acadian influence in New Orleans. The Spanish had some influence, especially with churches in Florida and the Southwest, but the British town plan and country estate had the biggest effect on the United States, beginning in the colonies up and down the Atlantic coast. With plenty of wood, colonists built from their memory of European wood construction. Design modifications came immediately after design problems were discovered. For instance, in New England, colonist builders added heavy siding to combat the wind and cold. Later, on the midwestern plains, sod, rammed earth, and brick took up where the trees left off.

As people moved and mingled in the melting pot, they brought their regional—mostly European—Old World heritage with them. Industrial cities that grew up in the late 1800s and early 1900s became patchwork compositions of identifiably ethnic neighborhoods. Toledo has a different climate from New Orleans, but they look different mostly because they have developed differently.

In the last part of the 1900s, instant communications and ever-more-rapid travel have been blurring regional and national distinctions. What was once a timber-frame house found mainly in New England became a New-England-style house available anywhere two-by-four framing materials could be shipped. A light-gray vinyl-sided, pitched shingled roof townhouse community is as much at home in Butte, Montana, as in Pensacola, Florida.

Even though there are still many regional variances, we are developing a national identity in our built environment, much of which is the result of technological leaps. The two-by-four frame house is a simple one that had a profound effect. The automobile has given us the everpresent garage, carport, or parking area, as well as circumferential highways, strip malls, and mobile homes. Telephones and electrification brought us telephone poles and wires. Advancements in electronic communications have given us satellite dishes and antennae. And computerization is making its own mark. Still, the future of each region is affected by its past and present. Cities look different from one another because change is constant but not consistent.

WHY ARE MOST ARCHITECTS MALE?

Architecture traditionally was (and, although it's hard to believe, still is) known as a "gentleman's profession." It is not an easy way to make a living; it requires long years of study and apprenticeship, and the pay for most is not commensurate with the hours and training, at least compared with other professions. Most architects don't reach even modest fame and fortune until their late thirties at the earliest, so it was best to be a gentleman with other means of support in the interim. Furthermore, until the late 1970s, the American Institute of Architects' Code of Ethics prohibited architects from advertising and marketing their services. This created difficulties for a newcomer trying to get work; one needed a network. Because most of the people already established in the field were male (and white), and (at least) middle-aged, and of (some) means, the sociological circle was rather closed. It has begun to break down somewhat, but all stereotypes die hard.

In the days of the buggywhip and the bustle, the rigorous engineering program that comprised a good portion of the architect's education was deemed too much for delicate female constitutions, and young girls were steered away from the field. And what employer wanted to hire a draftsperson who he knew would become pregnant and leave after he had labored so long to train her? But in architecture, as in most professions, there were pioneers to whom we all hold a debt.

Perhaps the best known of these women is Julia Morgan (1872–1957). Morgan has a long list of "firsts" attached to her name: first woman architect in the State of California, first woman to enroll in and graduate from Berkeley's engineering program (there was no architecture school in the western half of the United States at that time), first woman to gain acceptance in the Ecole des Beaux Arts in Paris (Morgan persevered for this honor through an unusual two years of entrance exams before her acceptance in 1898).

Morgan's career spanned almost half a century and 800 buildings (many in her native state of California) that include residential work, redesign of San Francisco's Fairmont Hotel after the 1906 earthquake, churches, and recreation centers for the newly formed Young Women's Christian Association, one of her steady clients. Another steady client was Phoebe Hearst, mother of newspaper tycoon William Randolph Hearst, who convinced her son to hire Morgan to design his estate at San Simeon atop a hill overlooking the Pacific Ocean. The resulting complex, which includes the huge castle ("Casa Grande") living space–art gallery, and three guest cottages, was constructed over a period of twenty years. Morgan's most publicized work, with its eclectic architecture and beautiful landscaping, today still wins the admiration of many a visitor and tourist.

Julia Morgan, by all accounts, was dedicated, persevering, and an excel-

Julia Morgan, a pioneer of American women in architecture, designed the Casa Grande and its beautiful San Simeon estate for William Randolph Hearst.

lent architect. Although the women following in her footsteps have an easier path because of the inroads she and others paved, acceptance of women into the profession has been slow. As late as 1955 noted architect Pietro Belluschi wrote, "I cannot, in whole conscience, recommend architecture as a profession for girls. I know some women who have done well at it, but the obstacles are so great that it takes an exceptional girl to make a go of it. If she insisted on becoming an architect, I would try to dissuade her. If then, she was still determined, I would give her my blessing—she could be that exceptional one."

The AIA Women in Architecture committee adopted "That Exceptional One" as the title for its 1988 traveling exhibition featuring the work of women architects, including Denise Scott Brown, Frances Halsband, Jane Goody, Cathy Simon, Jane Hastings, Beverly Willis, and Norma Skalek. The exhibition contains an eye-opening video in which the women present their views and experiences of the profession.

Even today, these women architects truly are "the exceptional ones." The American Institute of Architects—known by some as the original old boys' club—reported in 1988 that 2,000 regular members and 2,000 associate (non-registered-architect) members are women, which equals 8 percent of its total membership of 55,000. (Don't be appalled—in 1975, there were only 250 women members.) The figure actually may not be as low as it seems; 62 percent of all architects are AIA members. Of the 37 percent who have chosen not to join, more than 8 percent may be women who have not found sufficient reason to be members of the AIA.

With women entering professions such as medicine and law at something on the order of three and four times this rate, one wonders if the female best and brightest are looking for more lucrative careers, where acceptance is more firmly established.

ARE THERE ARCHITECTS IN OTHER COUNTRIES?

Architects outside the United States have different levels of responsibility and authority, depending on the customs and laws of each country. In most of the industrialized nations, though, architects are rather similar.

There are some differences. Even though "Herr Architect" carries the same respectful courtesy in Germanic countries as does "Herr Doktor," such is not quite the case in the United States. Likewise, although the

Architects in other countries must meet their nations' culture and ideals, exemplified by Minoru Takeyama's Ni-Ban-Kan commercial building in Tokyo.

architect has absolute authority on a job site in northern Africa, architects in the United States have relatively little authority during construction. But, because of a shared lineage that goes back to the master-builder craftsmen of the Middle Ages, architects around the world display a significant similarity of purpose and method.

In medieval times and earlier, large buildings were usually civic or religious and were designed by master craftsmen (often stone masons) who had learned their craft over the course of twenty or more years serving first as apprentice and then as a journeyman going from job site to job site for work. This method of training worked well because building systems often were a matter of long-standing tradition, buildings sometime took a lifetime to build, and accumulation of skills and knowledge in a predominantly illiterate society could also span a lifetime.

Things began to change as merchants established themselves in society alongside the two existing society-controlling estates: royalty and the church. Cities grew larger as did buildings for trade and commerce, and new building systems began to be introduced at an ever-increasing pace that is still racing along today. With more and more large, complex buildings, the apprentice-to-master-builder system gave considerable power to craft guilds.

At about the time of the Age of Reason in the eighteenth century, European royal families began reaffirming their power. Scholarship had become a pursuit sponsored by royalty, rather than by the churches alone, and education of master builders became the realm of royal educators and licensers rather than guildsmen.

In 1750 the Ecole des Beaux Arts—the French royal academy for sculpture, painting, and architecture established in 1671—began a separate school of architecture. The strict definition of an architect that developed soon after had a direct and profound effect on Architecture (with a capital A) in Europe, the Americas, and, eventually, most of the rest of the world.

The Industrial Age increased complexity because it introduced affordable steel for use in buildings, small motors for powering fans and elevators, sewage systems, and dozens of other innovations that we take for granted today, but which were instrumental in making industrial centers livable toward the end of the last century. Between the two world wars, ideas on the social responsibility of architects spread readily from Europe to the United States and back again. This was the age of the gentleman architect.

Gentlemen architects of the Bauhaus era (named after an architecture school started in post-World War I Germany) were concerned with making life more livable for the masses (see pp. 124–125). Like many who speak of "the masses," it could be argued that an unreasonably large number of Bauhaus disciples considered themselves well above that scrambling horde of uncouth, tasteless humanity. Nonetheless, the altruistic spirit prevailed and the ideas of precision of detail, simplicity of form, and economy of material were readily exported throughout Europe and the United States. And the modern movement of architecture took hold.

After World War II, housing and infrastructure (societal support systems such as hospitals, transportation facilities, sewers, government centers, and so on) were in severely short supply in Europe, while housing, industry, and commerce boomed in the United States. Both situations meant lots of work for building professionals, and architecture became a bonafide business venture as much as, or more than, a craft and intellectual pursuit. Because architecture developed throughout the industrialized nations at about the same pace and on a somewhat concurrent schedule over a period of a hundred years or more, architects around the world are similar in many more ways than they are different.

WHO WAS DANIEL H. BURNHAM?

"Make no small plans" is attributed to Daniel H. Burnham (1846–1912), who actually said, "Make no little plans, they have no magic to stir men's blood . . . Make big plans . . . remembering that a noble, logical diagram once recorded will never die but long after we are gone will be a living thing asserting itself with ever growing consistency."

Burnham lived out his philosophy by making big plans, which were, in fact, large enough to encompass entire cities. He is the acknowledged founder of the City Beautiful movement (1890s to 1920s) launched by the Chicago World Columbian Exposition in 1893. From this movement rose monumental civic buildings, often done in white marbles in neoclassical styles, surrounded by open public green spaces and graced with broad vistas. City Beautiful plans made their mark on Washington, D.C., Cleveland, San Francisco, and Manila in the newly acquired Philippines. Most notable in its completeness of the concept was the Chicago Plan of 1909, developed by Burnham and Edward H. Bennett.

Burnham also designed big buildings for his day, including the famed Rookery Building (1887) and Monadnock Building (1890) in Chicago, his hometown, and the Flat Iron Building in New York City (1903). His first job was with William LeBaron Jenney, king of the steel-framed skyscraper (see pp. 23–24), and his architectural partner was John Burnham Root.

The other side of Burnham's architectural coin were train stations in the beaux arts classical tradition, including Union Station in Pittsburgh (1902), Union Station in Washington, D.C. (1904), and Union Station in El Paso (1905). Notably, Union Station in Washington, D.C., was restored in 1988, making it truly a "living thing with ever growing consistency."

Daniel Burnham's Flat Iron Building in New York City was completed in 1903, just one example of his great plans.

137

WHO WAS BUCKMINSTER FULLER?

"You belong to the universe," was one of the watch phrases of Richard Buckminster Fuller, a.k.a. "Bucky," (1895–1983). Bucky's global, even universal, viewpoint disallows classification of his professional career: he was architect, engineer, inventor (who held twenty-eight patents), cartographer, editor, and writer all wrapped into one. Many of his creations encompassed what Fuller named the "Dymaxion" principle, which

Buckminster Fuller created an entire universe in one of the world's best known geodesic domes, the U.S. Pavilion at the 1967 Montreal Expo.

advocated designing for maximum use out of minimal energy and materials. Examples include the streamlined three-wheeled Dymaxion Car (exhibited at the 1933 Chicago World's Fair) that could turn on a dime and could sustain speeds of 120 miles per hour; the Dymaxion House, a hexagonal structure hung from a central mast by six cables, and the Dymaxion World map, with projection techniques that divide the earth's surface into triangles, avoiding distortion of any of the land areas common in traditionally projected maps.

Fuller's principles of maximum use with minimal expenditure of materials and energy perhaps are best demonstrated through his invention of the geodesic dome, patented in 1954. The surface of a geodesic dome is composed (of triangulated trusses of octohedrons and tetrahedrons, with linear elements forming great circles) in a way that distributes its structural load across the entire face of the dome. Therefore, the geodesic sphere is the only structure that gets stronger as it gets larger, and it has an unlimited span. Because of the way the load is distributed equally across its entire surface, its structural components need not get larger as the dome itself gets larger. To illustrate the economies of such a structure, consider this example: if you double the diameter of the dome, the enclosed space increases eight times, but the surface area increases only four times. Therefore, as the dome gets larger, there is proportionately less surface area to build. Less surface area means less building materials needed, less heat loss, and less maintenance per the enclosed volume. The dome's true economy of scale prompted Bucky to put forth the theory of covering entire cities with geodesic domes.

Although our cities to date remain exposed to the atmosphere, hundreds of thousands of geodesic domes dot the globe. For instance, the U.S. Navy has build "Radomes" all around the Arctic Circle to house radar equipment. Probably the most famous geodesic dome is the U.S. Pavilion at the Montreal Expo, designed in 1967 by Fuller and his architecture partner Shoji Sadao.

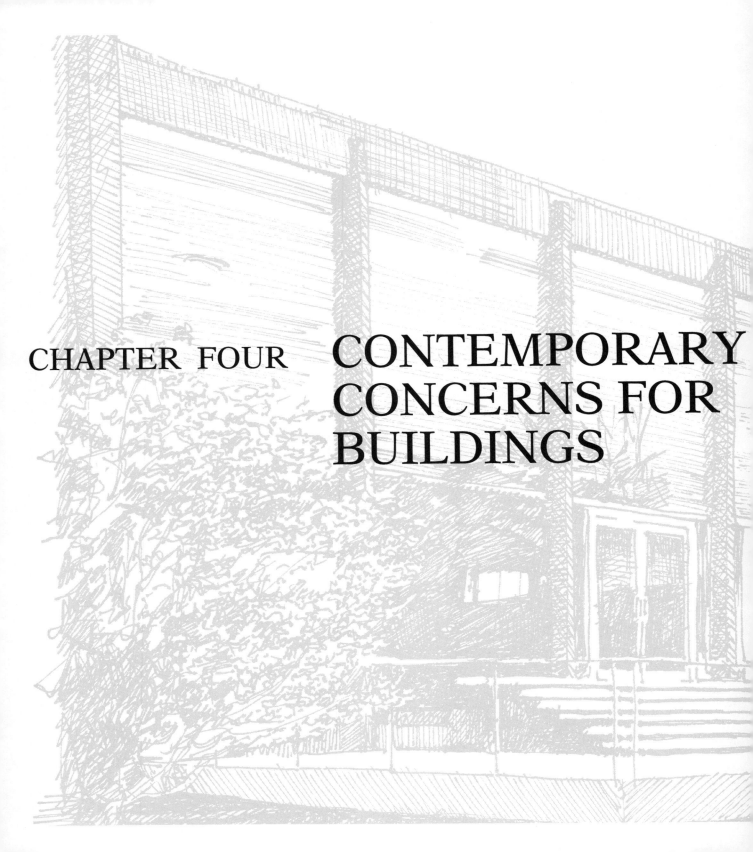

CHAPTER FOUR

CONTEMPORARY CONCERNS FOR BUILDINGS

Architect joke: Three professionals were to be guillotined during the French Revolution. The first on the block was a lawyer. The executioner pulled the rope and, mysteriously, the blade stopped inches from his neck. "Mon dieu, it is a miracle!" the executioner exclaimed. "Set the lawyer free!"

The second, a doctor, put his head on the block, the executioner pulled the rope, and lo and behold, again the blade stopped short. "Another miracle," the crowd shouted, "set the doctor free!"

Then the architect mounted the platform. He turned to the executioner and said, "You know, if you turn that eyebolt 90 degrees and shake the kink out of the rope, this thing will work just fine."

Architects want everything to work correctly, and have a sharp eye for details. In the money-driven, cut-throat world of real estate development, architects also seem all too often to have a minimal concern for their own well-being. It may be that the study of creating buildings that respond to human behavior and need instills in architects a fundamental sense of altruism. Then again, it may be that the schools and practices of architecture attract creative people who think of design problem solving ahead of their own physical concerns. At any rate, the result has been that architects have a lot of credibility among the public and often are looked up to as doers of public good, as well as the keepers of a public aesthetic.

In this section we will look at some of the areas in which architects are making a mark toward improving the way we live. Pollution, energy, concern for our aging population, making a fully active life possible for persons with disabilities, and, for that matter, making the built environment more comfortable and responsive to everyone's needs, are all goals of architecture.

What is "Sick Building Syndrome"?

Are your eyes, nose, and throat irritated? Do you suffer from allergylike symptoms, yet don't have allergies? Does your skin get red and irritated? Or is it a question of mental fatigue, memory loss, and reduced powers of concentration? Do these symptoms disappear if you are away from your job for twenty-four hours or longer? If so, it may be that it's not (as you have suspected all along) that you're sick of your job; it may be that your office is making you sick.

Sick building syndrome was first diagnosed in the late 1970s, and originally earned the moniker of "tight building syndrome," because many of its sufferers worked in new office buildings designed to be tight, that is, energy efficient. These well-insulated buildings allowed less air infiltration, so the same air lingered within an office. Couple this with more efficient standards for mechanical ventilating equipment that mandated fewer air changes per hour, and you have the perfect setup for airborne chemicals and contagions that cause sick building syndrome.

Sick building syndrome is usually not that difficult to pin down: It often occurs after office workers move to a new building or after a building renovation has taken place. However, diagnosing the source of the problem is another matter. In addition to generating inadequate air flow, mechanical systems can harbor toxic microorganisms, especially if they become wet or dirty. (This is the cause of the now infamous "Legionnaire's disease," one of the most deadly results of sick building syndrome.)

Other building components can contribute to this syndrome as well: any kind of plastic, fabrics on partitions, carpets, adhesives, ceiling tiles, paints, and coatings can all create a toxic atmosphere. Although legislation is in the works, manufacturers in most areas are not yet required to make the public aware of most of these chemical components.

The good news is that with increased concern and knowledge about indoor air pollution on the part of the public and the design professions, preventative measures are now available. Codes now require increased air changes per hour. Many architects are specifying products known to be hazard free. The number of public and private studies of sick building syndrome is increasing steadily. An experimental procedure, called *bakeout*, in which the temperature of a new or renovated building is elevated and maximum outside air introduced for a period of 24 hours, shows promise in removing a good portion of toxins before the building is occupied.

If you suspect your office is causing sick building syndrome, contact the nearest state or local Occupational Safety and Health Adminstration (OSHA) office, and request the proper forms to file a written complaint. (As a rule, OSHA offices will accept telephone complaints only on an emergency basis.) Any worker may file such a complaint, and his or her name can be held confidential, if requested.

One factor in sick building syndrome may be nonopenable windows, such as this typical highrise. When your building is sick, the best remedy usually is more fresh air.

143

WHAT IS THE ASBESTOS SCARE ALL ABOUT?

There are several different minerals that share a property that makes them helpful and harmful at the same time. These minerals are all called asbestos. They break up into tiny fireproof fibers that can be woven into cloth or added to binders to make fire-resistant clothing; curtains for theaters; backing for floor tiles; insulation and fire protection for furnaces, pipes, and structural steel; linings for brakes; felt for built-up roofing, tabletops resistant to laboratory chemicals; and fiber-reinforced concrete, to name just a few critical products that have incorporated ton upon ton of asbestos, mostly since World War II.

The asbestos scare comes from the fact that the tiny, inert fibers embed themselves in people's lungs and won't go away. Heavy exposure to fiber dust, even over a short period, has been proven to cause horrible maladies years later. One is asbestosis, also called white lung, in which the fibers have accumulated in the lungs and scarred them so badly that the sufferer no longer gets sufficient oxygen. The result is agonized suffication over a period of months or years. Another, much less common disease is mesothelioma, an excruciating tumorous growth of the lung lining, also fatal. We know these diseases stem from exposure to asbestos because although usually rare maladies, they have shown up with tragic frequency among asbestos miners and World War II shipbuilders (who worked in a constant haze of sprayed asbestos ship-hull insulation).

Asbestos removal, the last step in asbestos mitigation, is a dangerous and expensive process, to be avoided when possible.

The lawsuits and publicity related to the miners' and shipworkers' suffering led to federal laws that regulated the acceptable asbestos fiber level in a workspace. Even though there is no proof that low-level exposure to asbestos is harmful, the Environmental Protection Agency (EPA) established a specific number of fibers per cubic inch below which it considers the air to be acceptable and above which it does not (0.02 fibers per cubic centimeters of air). Based on simple, linear logic, the EPA set limits on asbestos fiber levels by first calculating what fiber levels caused how many cases of asbestos-related disease in miners and shipworkers. Then, working backward from that, technicians interpolated a fiber level at which fewer than one in one million people could be expected to contract an asbestos-related disease. The problem with that logic is twofold. For one thing, human organisms rarely react linearly (long-term low-level poisoning, for instance, may create a tolerance or it may accumulate to eventual death; it depends on the poison as well as the person). Second, the acceptable EPA levels considered for building interiors were lower than the outside air levels in some areas.

Asbestos dust is everywhere, and always has been, at least as long as animals have moved on the earth. In some locations, such as asbestos mining towns, research has indicated that long-term exposure to ambient-air asbestos levels much greater than required by EPA have no significant effect on the people living there (other than the miners exposed to the very high dust levels in the mines).

But whether asbestos poses the threat that lawmakers have been led to believe is not a matter open to debate. Asbestos, an inexpensive and extremely beneficial material in the past, is no longer allowed in building products. The law goes further, requiring containment and eventual removal of all asbestos in schools and government buildings. If the trend continues, the U.S. building industry will spend billions of dollars to clean up a situation that may not have been all that dirty in the first place.

It costs as much as 100 times as much to remove asbestos-containing materials in the controlled way dictated by law than it cost to put the asbestos in place initially. And even though regulations require extremely careful dust control during removal, the dust isn't visible and procedures for determining dust levels in air are imperfect. The result—especially with the panic for removal and omnipresence of at least a few unscrupulous contractors in any field—is that the widespread removal of asbestos could actually cause a short-term exposure for building occupants to rather high levels of asbestos dust during a sloppy asbestos removal job.

This is not to say that asbestos isn't harmful. Its harm in certain circumstances has been proven. This is one instance, however, where a little bit of careful consideration might have proved better than knee-jerk fervor when it came to banning a proven life-saving material (mostly against fire).

How can i protect against radon?

The first step in protecting against colorless, tasteless, odorless radon is to understand its nature and why it has become a "building horror" recently. Radon is the by-product of naturally occurring uranium in bedrock doing what it has always been doing—breaking down and releasing radioactive gases. If a person breathes radon, the release of its radioactive gases can cause serious lung damage. In fact, studies of uranium miners have linked high radon levels with lung cancer.

Over the past ten years, after the link was established, numerous studies have shown many areas of the country to have dangerously high radon levels. Perhaps most well-publicized of these is the "Reading Prong" of New Jersey and Pennsylvania (which is centered at Reading, Pennsylvania), where the underlying bedrock had a very high level of uranium.

Then, in 1988 the U.S. Environmental Protection Agency advised that all housing and light commercial buildings be tested for radon. This is the most prudent course of action, especially if one is contemplating purchase of a new home. Tests range from do-it-yourself, mail-in canisters to electronic tests done by professionals. Tests should first be conducted as close as possible to the ground (usually the cellar or basement), the most common point of entry for radon. Unless the tests for your building show a very high level of radon (over 200 picocuries per liter), don't panic. Remedial steps can usually be taken to mitigate radon in existing buildings.

Most of the steps are relatively inexpensive and easy. They all center on getting more fresh air into the building (especially buildings built in the past decade that were tightly sealed for energy conservation) and blocking common paths that radon follows to get into the building. Increasing natural or forced ventilation, especially in basements or crawl spaces, can help. Reducing negative pressure in these areas, mainly by adding makeup air for appliances that have exhaust systems (such as clothes dryers) will also help cut radon levels significantly. Sealing radon entry pathways—cracks in concrete, pipe penetrations, floor and wall joints, trench drains, and sump pumps—will stop the problem at its source. If higher levels of radon are present, a special radon vent can be installed under a basement slab. Such a vent will depressurize the ground beneath the slab, denying the radon a pathway for entry.

Of course, it is much easier to solve these problems before construction, and many designers currently take into account radon mitigation while building projects still are on the drawing boards. The methods used are similar to the ones described above, and involve sealing the possible radon pathways and providing plenty of ventilation air. Vapor barriers under the basement slab, waterproofing of outside walls, and poured concrete basement walls (instead of blocks, which create pathways unless they are capped) all should be part of a new house design in a radon-prone area. Even so, it doesn't hurt to perform radon testing after the building is completed.

External appearance is no clue to the presence of radon. Even innocent-looking homes may harbor the harmful, invisible gas. Radon can be mitigated through careful design (or redesign) that centers on getting fresh air into the building and blocking paths that radon uses to sneak in.

WHAT DOES IT MEAN TO FIREPROOF A BUILDING?

No building is fire*proof*. Fire resistance is built into buildings with the use of materials that do not contribute to flame spread, with materials that retard the spread of flame, and with fire-control mechanisms, such as sprinklers.

As a result of horribly destructive fires in cities cramped with wood buildings during the turn of the last century (including the great Chicago fire), laws governing the way buildings are designed and maintained have required fire-resistant features. At first, this meant including adequate exits and not building all-wood buildings in dense, inner-city locations. As the codes became more sophisticated, code requirements became more stringent.

A leading theory for making a building fire resistant these days is called compartmentalization. The idea is to break up a building into smaller areas with fire barriers in between. If you see a sign, "Fire Door, Keep Closed," you are looking at a compartmentalized fire-control system. Part of this strategy is to rate building systems as to the time it takes for fire to pass from one side to another. For instance a two-hour fire door is about the safest door available commercially, and is probably made of hollow steel without a window (or, if there is a window, it is small and contains wire mesh).

Taking the compartmentalization concept a step farther is the concept of creating safe areas of refuge. The idea is to create a safe path through which people may evacuate a building, or create a place where the heat and smoke will not build up to dangerous levels during a building fire.

It is smoke, not flame, that most endangers life during a fire. More deaths are caused by asphyxiation from smoke than from heat during fires, which is especially true for the toxic smoke that comes from many man-made materials. A positive-air-pressure stairwell is an example of an area of refuge from both flame and smoke. Fire-resistant doors lead to a concrete-, masonry-, or gypsum-lined stairwell into which a fan pumps outside air. While fire is delayed from getting into the stairwell, the positive air pressure keeps smoke out, too.

One problem with compartmentalization is that it depends on there being no gaps between fire compartments, and on there being no human error. For instance, if someone props open a fire door, it is useless for its intended purpose. Open windows likewise create the possibility that fire will climb from one floor to the next outside the building. Or, if there is a floor-to-floor gap, such as a hole drilled through the floor for wiring, and the hole is not protected, smoke and fire will find their way from one floor to another inside the building.

To help smoke barriers work better, manufacturers have developed a number of fire retardants and smoke blockers. Chemical treatment of

Even steel-frame construction such as that in New York's World Trade Center (architect Minoru Yamasaki) cannot withstand the heat of a large fire, and must be fire-proofed.

fabrics is one example. When flame is applied, the fabric tends to blacken and give off relatively harmless gases. But when the flame is removed, the fabric stops burning.

Some materials *intumesce*. This means that they swell when they are heated, which forms a fireproof barrier on the material to be protected. Intumescent paints have been shown to make wood an acceptable fire-resistant material for some code jurisdictions. Intumescent putties and other fillers allow the builder to run plastic pipe through fire-barrier penetrations without worry. When fire melts away the plastic, the heat also swells the intumescent material, closing the resulting hole. Intumescents are also a boon for applications where limited space is available, for instance coating steel where there isn't enough room for gypsum sheathing or spray-on fireproofing.

Fire-proofing steel? Yes, the steel in buildings must be fireproofed too. Building fires can easily climb to 1,700 degrees Fahrenheit and more. At these temperatures, the structural strength of steel is diminished to the point that it may not be able to hold up the loads for which it was designed. The result may be partial or complete building collapse.

Another strategy for making buildings fire resistant—aside from compartmentalization—is sprinklering. Water, either from holding tanks on the building roof or from municipal water mains, feeds into pipes laid into the ceiling. Water spigots located at regular intervals along the water pipes are typically activated when an easily melted switch holder is heated by flame. During a fire, the switches trip and the water flows, retarding or extinguishing the fire. Sprinklers have been around for a long time, especially in warehouses and fire-exit areas, and they have proven themselves particularly effective as a fire-control mechanism.

Even newer in the panoply of fire-control strategies and devices at the command of architects is something called a smart building. Electronic controls are at the heart of a smart building. Computer monitors help building maintenance personnel detect fires at an early stage. The remote detection devices may sound alarms, call the fire department, activate positive-air fans, close fire doors, and bring all the elevators to the ground floor. (If you've ever wondered why signs tell you not to use elevators during a fire, it's because elevator shafts are among the first places that fill up with smoke during a fire.) Smart buildings help make fire-resistant building systems a little more resistant to human error and, thus, a little safer (see pp. 164–165).

There is no such thing as a fireproof building. But with the help of lawmakers, design professionals, and product manufacturers, buildings—and the people in them—are getting a bit safer all the time.

Why are buildings tied to environmental concerns?

"Pollution is a resource out of place," Charles Howell proclaimed in May 1990, at a conference held in Washington, D.C., soon after the twentieth anniversary of Earth Day. The statement and the meeting are signs of a new attitude growing within the design professions. At a time when non-renewable resources, such as oil, are causes for worldwide conflict, and even renewable resources, such as old-growth timber, are disappearing from the marketplace, we are all realizing the importance of conservation and environmental sensitivity.

Architects and engineers, in particular, are coming to appreciate that the construction industry is a major consumer of resources and is in need of environmentally sensitive design. Developers too will begin to realize that environmental sensitivity is good business when their tenants and buyers demand it.

Environmental sensitivity means energy, water, and soil conservation as a concern during the design and construction of buildings. It also means concern for the environmental impact of producing and transporting building materials. Does the use of aluminum from Guyana mean destruction of the South American rain forest to mine it? Are rare hardwoods from Cameroon taken at the expense of the African rain forest? Is the processing of certain types of insulation wreaking havoc with our ozone layer? And what about the effect on building occupants when volatile organic compounds pollute indoor air, such as the formaldehyde used as a glue solvent in processing fiberboard and carpeting? And finally, are the materials chosen for construction going to be recyclable when the building, eventually, is demolished?

These and other questions do not provide one simple answer. Trade-offs are necessary and compromises inevitable. The overall direction is positive, though, because people are genuinely concerned with the state of the environment and believe that existing strategies and technologies, if widely used in practice, will benefit the environment over the long run.

In the home, ventilation and solar orientation are two aspects of environmentally sensitive design that have a major impact on energy use and the comfort, health, and well-being of the occupants. Ventilation means lots of air circulation from the outside. Because heating and air conditioning use energy, heat has to stay in or out, depending on the weather, while air flows in and out freely. This may seem an impossible trick, but it is easily accomplished with heat exchangers, which take the heat out of the air going in one direction, inside or outside, and reapply it to the air going in the other direction.

Ventilation and orientation are also important in large office and commercial buildings. With large buildings, interior lighting is a major energy and comfort concern too. The lighting industry has responded by developing lights that are cool, energy-efficient, and of colors and intensities that mimic natural lighting. The designer weighs their extra cost against their long-term benefits.

Construction is the realm of the contractor, but design professionals can still have a major impact on its environmental sensitivity. Erosion of

Buildings can be large consumers of energy and producers of waste, or can gently harmonize with the environment, as do the pueblos of Mesa Verde in southwest Colorado.

bulldozed earth may be the biggest concern. A soils engineer can advise the architect and owner on how to minimize erosion and impact on the water table through proper construction sequencing, ground covers, subground treatment, and other guidelines for the contractor's work later.

Another construction despoiler is spillage and improper disposal of harmful chemicals, such as one finds in some paints and cleaning compounds. Laws, like those in California, sometimes limit the materials that may be used to those that have the least environmental impact. Attention to wind, runoff, application methods, and proper disposal is the responsibility of an environmentally sensitive contractor.

Protection of trees and endangered animals may also be an issue. What once was looked at as useless swamp that should be drained, now must be seen as valuable wetlands harboring a storehouse of genetic variety in the form of plants and animals. The complex interrelationship between nature and humans possibly makes these areas valuable to us for our sake. But we are all coming to the realization that nature is valuable for its own sake, and only humans have the power to choose whether to preserve and maintain, or to change and destroy.

Residential and commercial buildings use about 36 percent of the energy consumed in this country, with another 15 percent going into the construction of buildings. In other words, over half of our energy supply goes into constructing and operating buildings—heating, air conditioning, and electrical needs for machinery and lighting. (Another major chunk, 27 percent, of the total energy consumed goes toward transportation.) Before the oil embargo of 1972, our buildings were becoming energy pigs. It didn't matter too much that high-rise glass boxes leaked air like sieves, or that mechanical equipment was inefficient, or that office layouts were designed with twice as much lighting as they needed—energy was abundant and cheap.

While waiting in line for gasoline during the early seventies, we had plenty of time to rethink these notions. Just as the automobile industry began to manufacture small, gas-efficient cars, architects and the rest of the building industry began producing energy-efficient architecture. A felicitous consequence of the energy crisis is that our buildings are much more energy conserving than those of just ten years ago.

All types of buildings, from offices to houses, are much better insulated and weather sealed to control flow of heat in and out of the building. Double-glazing and different types of heat-reflecting glass are common for commercial buildings (see pp. 31–32), to avoid unwanted heat buildup that makes air-conditioning systems work harder. Lighting systems, on average, use 30 percent less electricity than those of a decade ago. Mechanical equipment (and its smaller counterparts, household appliances) are rated and labeled for energy efficiency, which has become a major selling point. This has come about in part because of stricter building codes and consumer protection laws, and simple avoidance of high operating costs. But one could not discount plain old aversion to wastefulness, once people's eyes were opened.

Architects rediscovered simple precepts that were important to designers before the days of cheap energy. Southern orientations for buildings can bring in free natural light and heat. Well-placed trees and overhangs can block out unwanted glare and sun. Openable windows located in the right place in a house can induce cross-ventilation, maybe even enough to disallow the air conditioner. Solar energy caused headlines in the 1970s, especially for residential building. The concept is appealing—free energy from the sun used to heat water (or to heat space directly).

Many of these first residential solar energy systems were called active systems, which means they require mechanical parts to keep them working. The collector panels, placed to face south, that appeared on many house roofs were often parts of active systems. A fluid in the panels was heated by the sun and pumped into the house, where it in turn (through heat exchangers) heated the domestic water for bathing and cooking, or for steam heating. Two of the reasons that these systems did not achieve great popularity were that they required pumps and holding tanks that, first, were expensive, and, second, needed continual maintenance.

Passive systems, with no major mechanical parts, rapidly replaced active systems as a concept for capturing the sun's energy. Although some

The energy crisis of the 1970s forced architects to reconsider some of the "old ways" of design, including natural ventilation, shutters for shading, and masonry construction, which moderates heat gain and loss.

used collector panels, most work on the concept of letting the sun directly into the space, capturing its heat in the mass of a wall or floor, and letting the mass release the heat in the cooler nighttime hours. Sometimes the mass is a specially built wall called a *trombe wall*, which faces south and is painted black or covered with glass to enable it to store more heat and slow down its release. Using insulation, window shades, blinds, overhangs, air vents or openable windows in passively heated spaces, the occupant can control the heat in the house. (If this sounds like a ridiculously simple idea, that's because it is. It has been around since Vitruvius in Greece and since the pueblos of the American Southwest. If your house has a sunroom with shades over the windows, you have a simple type of passive system. Fine-tuning the controls and balancing the amount of mass in the room just make it work more efficiently.)

Photovoltaics are most likely the solar energy system of the future. Wafer-thin cells made of silicone generate direct-current electricity when placed in the sun. Put enough of them together, and you can meet all the energy needs of a building through electricity. The major drawback to photovoltaic systems has been their expense; when they were first developed, they could only produce electricity at hundreds of times the cost of fossil fuel systems. Today, the cost is within three or four times the cost of a fossil fuel system, to the point that photovoltaics can be used more cost effectively than traditional systems in remote areas, where the cost of bringing the electrical grid to a location is high. (For this reason, photovoltaic systems are rapidly gaining popularity in many developing countries.) A clue to their imminent acceptance is that major oil companies currently are funding their research and development, looking perhaps, for a way to meter the sun?

Regardless of the era of good energy feeling we experienced in the late 1980s, the energy crisis did not (and will not) go away, given the current form of most of our energy resources. Fossil fuels—oil, coal, and gas—are nonrenewable resources, meaning that once they are used up, there just is no more. That knowledge makes the use of renewable sources, including wind, sun, water, geothermal, and tidal power especially attractive. Renewable energy resources lack widespread use basically because of economics; while none of these renewable resources has yet proven to be as cheap as fossil fuels, costs are coming down as research and development yield more efficient ways to harness their use. Furthermore, you may have noticed that over the years your fuel bills have not been showing lower costs per unit of fuel due. Sooner or later, the cost of renewables will hit the break-even point with fossil fuels, and many experts predict their use will rapidly become widespread. Let's hope it happens before major fuel shortages occur, the ramifications of which are the stuff of nightmares.

How does the architect make life easier for people with disabilities?

One of the guidebooks used by architects for designing barrier-free environments reminds them that all people have physical disabilities at some time in their lives. Nothing more quickly makes the usually able-bodied person realize how difficult navigating the built environment can be than a temporary disability. The young woman who is eight months pregnant knows; so do the teenager who broke his leg on the class ski trip and the little kid who is not tall enough to reach the doorknob. The middle-aged executive who just had drops placed in her eyes for a vision exam would agree, and none of them would get any argument from people with more permanent disabilities.

The Americans with Disabilities Act of 1990 requires that building owners make buildings accessible to persons with disabilities. One example is providing a ramp to an entrance that formerly could be reached only by climbing steps.

One of the first examples of barrier-free architecture is providing accessibility for persons in wheelchairs. Consider a scenario of how to design for a person in a wheelchair going to work in an office building. First, the parking space has to be wide enough to allow for both removal of the chair from the car and for the person to get into the chair. (That's 9 feet wide as opposed to a standard 5-foot-wide parking space.) The sidewalk curbs have to be cut wide enough and have a shallow enough slope for wheeling onto the sidewalk. If the entrance is elevated and reached by an ambulatory person via steps, a ramp that slopes less than 1 foot in every 12 feet of length will allow the disabled employee to get to the doorway. The door itself has to open automatically or have a knob and handle that can be worked from a sitting position, and the space must be wide enough (32 inches) to maneuver through.

The wheelchair user is now through the door, and the architect's responsibility for providing accessibility continues. Corridors must be wide enough for the chair; desks, public telephones, and drinking fountains must be at certain set heights. Accessible sinks and toilet stalls with wide doors, grab bars, and enough space to turn a chair around are required in public bathrooms. The next time you are in a public bathroom, check out the placement of sinks, towel holders, mirrors, soap dishes (and sanitary napkin dispensers, if you are female), and think about the inconvenience that would be caused by not being able to reach them.

Barrier-free design in its purest sense means building access for everyone. In addition to wheelchair users, this includes people with ambulatory disorders, blind people and those with impaired vision, and the hearing impaired. The first federal statute requiring that buildings (built with federal money) be accessible is the Architectural Barriers Act of 1968. Twenty years later every state has laws on its books requiring all state and public buildings in most classifications to be barrier free. With the passage of the Fair Housing Act and the Americans with Disabilities Act in 1990, barrier-free access to all public buildings is a legal right.

Architects now have at their disposal a host of design techniques that can make dealing with the built environment easier for all of us, and more and more of them are being applied to new and old buildings alike.

An aside about language: People with disabilities may take umbrage at being referred to as "handicapped." Think about it . . . we are only handicapped if physical and environmental barriers make us so.

HOW DOES THE ARCHITECT MAKE LIFE EASIER FOR ELDERLY PEOPLE?

By the year 2000, there will be 51 million more Americans than there were in 1980. The population of the United States will have increased 3.5 times since 1900, and there will be 11.5 times more Americans over age 65. With aging often come decreased mobility; strength and stamina; lessening of visual, hearing, and tactile ability; as well as cognitive impairment. All of these features can have an effect on the way housing for the elderly is designed, and many of them overlap with designing for universal access. They range from providing grab bars in bathrooms and slip-resistant floor surfaces (both for easier and safer mobility) to avoiding poorly lighted and repetitious corridors for easily disoriented users of multifamily housing.

In addition to small changes in everday residences, architects design special types of facilities to house the elderly, including congregate housing and "granny flats."

As just one example, designing the lighting for elderly people encompasses a special sensitivity to their needs. A 60-year-old person, with normal vision for his or her age, requires twice the level of light (illumination) as does the normal 20-year-old. Yet sensitivity to glare also increases with age. This means that the architect must consider providing a high level of indirect light, possibly with white ceilings and light-colored walls and furniture finishes. Windows should have some sort of shade or curtain to block glare from direct sun. Adjustable task lighting can supplement for activities that need close work, such as reading, sewing, or preparing food. Light bulbs and controls should be easy to reach and change, from a wheelchair if necessary.

On a larger scale, architects have recently begun to explore care for the elderly on a community level. As an alternative to nursing homes, continuing care retirement communities are becoming popular. These communities permit residents to live a totally independent life-style while they are mobile and active, and offer a wide range of support services, including senior activity centers, housekeeping and "meals on wheels," and medical facilities as needed. A typical continuing care retirement community supports 300 to 500 residents in single-family houses or apartments.

Other types of elderly housing that are rising in popularity include group homes (similar to boarding houses, with private bedrooms and shared kitchens, bathrooms, and living areas) and "granny flats," which are small, separate houses built on the land of an existing house, allowing Granny (or Gramps) a lot of freedom and privacy with occasional support of the family in the main house. The granny flat concept was introduced in Australia, where a prefabricated house, owned by the local government, was erected on the property of anyone who needed housing for an elderly relative.

Officially, a historic building is one listed on the National Register of Historic Places, which currently contains some 50,000 properties. A historic listing does not have to be for a single building—it can cover an entire district in a city or a single object within the building. Buildings don't have to be very old to be considered historic; Frank Lloyd Wright's Guggenheim Museum in New York City, completed in 1961, is a good example. Likewise, buildings don't have to be sterling examples of great architecture; "George Washington slept here" may be enough to qualify a building for a historic status.

Although the importance of preserving valued buildings dates back to ancient Roman times, the concept of historic preservation in the United States became particularly popular in the 1960s and 1970s, when a public social consciousness seemed to hit many arenas. Since this time, various techniques for making old buildings useful have evolved into discreet methodologies, each with its own name. Historic preservation, the purest form of the art, means protecting and maintaining the building in its existing state. An example is the Parthenon in Athens, which is treated to avoid further damage, yet was not added to or rebuilt. Restoration connotes returning the building as close as possible to its original condition, such as was accomplished with Thomas Jefferson's Monticello in Charlottesville, Virginia. Rehabilitation means remodeling to extend a building's useful life. If an office building has new storm windows installed, access floors added for wiring, and its interior walls moved to different places, it has been rehabilitated. Adaptive use entails changing the function of the building, again for the purpose of extending a building's useful life. Warehouses turned into apartments are one example; a railroad station turned into a restaurant is another.

These techniques may also be combined, as evidenced in Washington, D.C.'s Union Station, built in 1903 by architect Daniel Burnham (see pp. 136–137), closed in the early 1970s as a result of deterioration caused by neglect, and reopened in renewed glory in 1988. The main halls and function rooms of the train station were meticulously restored to their original magnificent materials and finishes by the architecture firm of Harry Weese and Associates. Concurrently, numerous shops, restaurants, and a multiscreen movie theater were designed on a newly created second level and in the basement by the architecture firm of Benjamin Thompson & Associates, making the "new" Union Station an adaptive use project as well.

With renewed public interest in saving and reusing old buildings has come a system of tax credits. To qualify for these tax credits, a building must be a "certified historic structure," listed individually in the National Register of Historic Places, or be located in a registered historic district

The City of Charleston, South Carolina, was designated the first historic district in the United States.

and certified as a significant contribution to that district. The Interior Department, which oversees the National Register, has developed a set of guidelines for how these structures shall be treated.

Although interest in restoring buildings is currently at an all-time high in this country, earlier milestones of preservation work deserve note. Many of the first efforts were privately funded, including development of a foundation to preserve George Washington's home at Mount Vernon, Virginia in 1856. Restoration of Colonial Williamsburg, begun in 1926, also took place under the auspices of private money.

The federal government became interested in the preservation business shortly thereafter, and most of its programs, then and now, are governed through the Department of Interior's National Park Service. For instance, the Historic American Buildings Survey (HABS) was established in 1935 to document important buildings for the Library of Congress. A year later, the first historic district, in Charleston, South Carolina, was declared.

Side by side with federal programs exist state preservation organizations, and local historic preservation boards, which often manifest themselves through local zoning ordinances. Even today, we cannot overlook the importance of private preservation organizations, the most influential of which is the National Trust for Historic Preservation. Such interest also extends beyond national borders, through international societies that exist for preservation of historic properties worldwide. Many of organizations operate under UNESCO, the United Nations Education, Scientific, and Cultural Organization.

(It is proper to say "a historic" building. It is improper to say "an historic" building, unless you are Queen Elizabeth, or someone speaking her English, and you drop your h's. Also, the proper terminology is "adaptive use," not "adaptive reuse," which is redundant and drives preservationists to tears.)

WHAT IS A SMART BUILDING?

In a way, it's like asking, "What is a smart person?" and the answer depends on your definition of "smart." Suffice it to say, however, that a smart building is one that electronically anticipates the needs of its occupants, and adjusts itself accordingly. Most office buildings built today are "smart" in a real-estate-selling sense of the word, meaning that they include or can accommodate a large network of electronic systems for telecommunications, computers, heating/cooling systems, and security.

The basic concept behind a smart building is that its sensors, located throughout the building, collect data about the building's environmental conditions and send them back to a computer, which processes the information and adjusts the building's systems. A simple example has to do with heating and cooling. If a thermometer (a heat sensor) measures a temperature of 60 degrees in the building basement, it sends that information to the computer, which in turn switches on the furnace and directs heated air through ducts to the basement. A more complex example is a fire safety system. A sensor measuring either heat or smoke might send the information to a computer, which in turn might call the fire department and tell in which part of the building the fire is located, bring all the elevators to the ground floor and keep them there, sound an alarm within the building, pressurize the stairways to drive smoke out, and activate sprinkler systems in the area of the fire. Pretty smart for a building, wouldn't you say?

Houses also are getting smarter all the time. Electric lights and appliances can already be programmed to turn on and off automatically at preset times. The "real" smart house, according to the prototype developed by the National Association of Home Builders Research Foundation, will have a new kind of integrated wiring system that accommodates power, communications, and audiovideo signals. All the components will be able to interact using the same language through a central computer. The components for making a house this smart already exist; it remains to be seen whether it will receive the necessary cooperation among manufacturers of various appliances and components and market acceptance.

Some of the features of the smart house: All outlets are for any device —the telephone and the TV can be plugged into the same place; lights turn on and off automatically by sensing whether there is a person in the room; a computer display tells if something is awry, for instance if the refrigerator door is open or the front door is unlocked; alarms are activated if an intruder enters; the entire system can be controlled from one location in the house, as well as remotely by telephone; the oven can be told to start roasting the chicken, and the heating or air conditioning can be programmed to turn on, say, half an hour before you come home from work. It is not yet programmed to fetch your pipe and slippers, but then, what else would be left for you (or your cocker spaniel) to do?

Liberty Center in downtown Pittsburgh, by UDA Architects, is a smart building, which integrates its fire alarm, smoke control, security, and mechanical systems.

Architects, as a whole, have been rather slow getting into the computer revolution. Many architects have resisted the notion that a computer can help with design. The argument is that one cannot automate a creative process. It is becoming obvious, though, that computers can relieve architects of much drudgery and increase the amount of time they have to devote to the creative processes of problem analysis and design synthesis. By the beginning of the nineties, about three-quarters of all architecture firms owned computer-aided design and drafting (CADD) equipment and over 90 percent had computers helping on non-design-related tasks. That's quite an increase from a decade earlier, when very few architects had any type of computer and almost none had CADD.

The foundations of computer-aided design, though, were established by professionals other than architects. From the first days of electronic information processing machines, engineers have jumped at the chance to use computers to make their work simpler. As microchip development began to make small, relatively powerful computers widely available, other professionals saw the digital light. And it wasn't only accountants and other number crunchers who found small computers indispensable in their race to be competitive. Just about every office environment, from auto-repair shops to corporate executive suites, benefited from data management, spreadsheet, and word processing software that turned personal computers into critical clerical resources.

Word processing and maybe some financial management were about as far as any computerization went in most architecture firms until the second half of the 1980s. Even in the 1970s, there was CADD software on the market, but architects weren't interested because early CADD systems were either too expensive or too primitive for architectural applications. Computer-aided design was first developed for nonarchitectural tasks. Automobile manufacturers or computer-chip designers, for example, could afford the expensive hardware and software that was necessary in the 1970s to devise shapes on the computer screen and conduct simulated tests. Architecture is even more complicated, and the typical one-to-three-person architecture firm has far less money to spend on equipment than, say, your typical auto conglomerate.

In the early 1980s, a number of large architecture firms made the decision to computerize their drafting. Computers costing $500,000 apiece, running software with a $10,000 price tag, somehow were magically supposed to make the work of architects easier. The systems, designed mostly for industrial engineers, couldn't do what architects wanted (at least not without a lot of training and hands-on experience, which was too time consuming for most busy design professionals). Stories were rampant of

Skidmore, Owings & Merrill, one of the largest architecture firms in the country, used computers in every phase of the 1990 design of Worldwide Plaza in New York City.

offices with half a million dollars worth of CADD equipment gathering dust in a closet.

Architecture is a small market for CADD manufacturers, but some of them paid attention to what architects said they needed and began to deliver at affordable prices. At first, simple drawing things—like easy placement of windows and doors and quick manipulation of lines and shapes—were the big obstacles. Development was fast because that's the way competition is in the computer market. Soon, architects were demanding three-dimensional (3D) design, and they weren't satisfied with 3D drawings on a flat surface. They wanted drawings that could be rotated by the computer to show hidden views, zoom-ins, and fly-arounds. They wanted the computer to calculate all light reflections in a drawing so that their full-color computer printouts would look like photographs instead of drawings. Architects wanted the computer to keep track of the materials necessary for construction, their cost, and ordering information. They've gotten all that, and now architecture is gaining the benefits of computerization.

But there is another side to the influence of computers on architecture. Because the machines are everywhere now, they have become an important design consideration in their own right. They take up a significant percentage of the energy consumed in many office buildings, collectively they create a lot of heat, they have to fit within the workspace and (hopefully) look reasonably attractive, lighting and screen placement have to minimize glare and allow good posture for the operator, and they require special communications hookups and a steady supply of clean power. These are all things architects must think about as they sit at their CADD stations. So there you have it—computers are helping architects design better environments for other computers.

WHY ARE OUR TALLEST SKYSCRAPERS ONLY A LITTLE MORE THAN A HUNDRED STORIES TALL?

When you think about the building technologies we have available today, it seems obvious that we should be able to build skyscrapers much taller than we have. This is true—we have the technical capacity to design a building two times higher than the tallest buildings in the world today, and more. Indeed, more than one of our best structural engineers today

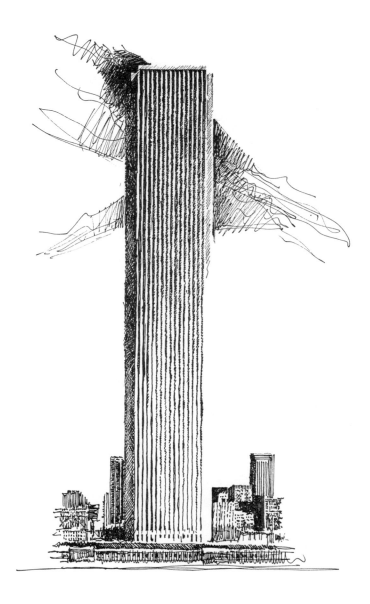

Skyscrapers are limited in height by building codes, the speed of elevators, and people's ability to tolerate swaying caused by wind pressure.

have the models and the drawings ready and waiting in their offices. The setbacks are basically questions of human comfort and economics.

First of all, there is the problem of wind-induced motion at very tall heights. The proposed structural systems for very tall buildings will make them strong enough that they don't fall down, even with the very strong winds that blow at that height. But such buildings are not likely to be stiff enough to avoid swaying dramatically in the wind. Building sway already occurs in the tall buildings now standing, although usually not enough to notice. With very tall buildings, though, sway might exceed 50 feet back and forth every 20 seconds. Even though the building itself would be safe from falling down under such punishment, people would probably be uncomfortable.

A second problem with very tall buildings is the question of providing vertical transportation to the upper floors. The number of elevator shafts necessary to transport people often eats up too much rentable space to make such a project financially worthwhile. Furthermore, an elevator can't travel at more than 20 miles per hour without passengers getting dizzy. Because the trip to the top would have to be broken down into several elevator rides (each ride meaning you must wait for another elevator) it's a long journey at 20 mph.

Third is the issue of the effect very tall buildings have on the surrounding neighborhood, in terms of gigantic building shadows, potential traffic jams of people traveling to and from the building (the World Trade Center supports more people than the entire population of Schenectady, New York), and the relative permanence of a skyscraper once it is built. All this is not to say that mile-high buildings will never happen. After all, having the tallest building in the world seems to be a matter of civic pride, and there are many city councils that might be willing to overlook a shadow that covers more than 100 acres.

I THINK A LOT OF BUILDINGS TODAY ARE UGLY. DO I HAVE BAD TASTE?

The best answer is "Everybody has bad taste but you and me, and sometimes I wonder about you." By definition, beauty is in the eye of the beholder, of course, and there is no such thing as bad taste. But in the eye of the world of high design, it isn't so much good or bad taste that matters as much as sophisticated taste.

There are reasons that most office buildings today look simple and cleanly defined (boxes with windows), that the AT&T Building in New York City looks like a Chippendale highboy (and like the body of a telephone), that the Portland Building in Oregon looks like an Egyptian artifact (or a color-blind conventioneer in his best polyesters), and that the design for the renovation of Times Square tears down the notion of perfect harmony and order and celebrates the confusion and vitality of that center circus ring in New York City (it looks like a mess, but on purpose). The problem for most of us is that we really don't understand what those reasons are.

Architects, like everybody else, want to be recognized as the best at what they do. But defining quality in buildings has long been a problem. One might be inclined to design the way the client wants. But, in an area as complex as building design and construction, the client is too easily influenced by factors with little bearing on quality: outdoing one's neighbor or competitor, for example, or enrobing one's building in trappings of glory that have nothing to do with the new building's purpose.

Defining a quality building as one that works best for the building users (rather than just the owner) is another possibility. But that is a very tough quality to measure and it changes. Knowing, for instance, that a wide glass door facing a major street makes it easier for visitors to find the place might easily be offset for regular occupants by uncomfortable solar heat gain in the lobby, or unbearable noise from the thoroughfare outside. Although function and comfort are very important, there is more to quality design than that.

The building's appearance, as already mentioned, isn't something that can be judged impartially either. We all know what we like; we just don't all agree.

On a larger scale, the building must fit well into the existing and future fabric of its surroundings. So another qualitative test is whether a building enhances its surroundings, detracts from them, or is neutral. And that judgment, again, rests with the individual. If you don't think woodland needs enhancement, you are going to think differently from someone who revels in the wonders of life in the wild.

What seems to have happened in the realm of building criticism, then, is that there are as many ideas of what quality design is as there are design

If you think some of today's buildings are ugly, you definitely do not have bad taste!

critics (maybe more). Furthermore, criticism of professionals whose work blends craft, science, and art, often leans toward attempts to more clearly define the gray areas. So, often, criticism of architecture is overshadowed by discussion of the art within design. Craft and science take a back seat.

The unfortunate result over the past forty or fifty years has been a long, highly publicized series of carefully constructed theories—generally worked out in college and often held throughout life—of what looks good. Attention to what works well and lasts with reasonable maintenance is critical to good design. But too often, technical precision just isn't as exciting to budding architects as the theory of form. In other words, style has become very important in architecture toward the goals of self fulfill-ment and peer recognition. Individuals and small groups of individuals have worked so feverishly and long to develop their own recognized style, that the race to be different can become more important, in some circles, than the race for overall quality.

In this world of high design, strange pieces hanging on avant garde forms aren't a sign of a stupid or lazy designer. Quite to the contrary, they are very carefully thought out allusions that either mock or celebrate something that has caught that designer's fancy, applied within the con-straints of some ism. If critics pick up on the "wittiness" of those illusions, the designer is likely to use them again, in which case they become part of that person's "design vocabulary." Without some care and oversight (by building owners, planning boards, citizen groups, critics, and architects alike), the clamor of individual design vocabularies vying for attention can easily become an unbearable babel of incomprehensible buildings that most would consider just plain ugly.

To further complicate matters, when one language of architecture does finally seem to emerge from the madness, it is then traditional design and, for that very reason, more likely to be overthrown than supported. Un-usual as it may sound, this is probably a good thing about contemporary design trends. New things are interesting to bright young people. Heady philosophizing is a form of recreation for budding genius. And the best way to attract the best minds to the pursuit of architectural study is to lure them with new ideas and deep pontification.

Because of their power over the viability and future direction of archi-tecture, those architects who inspire others have perhaps the greatest burden to bear of all those involved in defining architectural quality. Ar-chitecture is a relatively small field. So it is reasonably likely that a bright, hard-working individual can gain some level of personal recognition as an architect within his or her lifetime. Ultimately, though, landmark archi-tecture is judged over much more than one lifetime.

WHO WAS MIES VAN DER ROHE?

"Less is more," was one of the principles of Mies van der Rohe, clearly demonstrated in the twenty-six-story tall perpendicular towers of the Lake Shore Drive apartments in Chicago (1951) and the Seagram Building in New York City (1955). Both of these projects are prototypical "Mies" buildings, with open ground levels and flexible floor plans grouped around a service core. His curtain-wall building design and detailing, copied countless times by other architects, rarely is matched in quality. Mies's excellence as a craftsman of details in part may be attributable to his family's business of stonecutting, in which he took part as a young man.

Perhaps the most well known of all Mies's designs is the Barcelona Pavilion (which in reality was the German Pavilion of an international exhibition held at Barcelona, Spain, in 1929). Exteriors and interiors were designed by Mies, including the "Barcelona chair," still a best-selling classic today.

Ludwig Mies van der Rohe proved that less is more with his elegant design of Crown Hall, built in 1956 on the Illinois Institute of Technology campus.

Who is Robert Venturi?

"Less is a bore," said Robert Venturi, who in 1966 authored *Complexity and Contradiction in Architecture,* the book that dropped the bomb on modern architecture. Venturi said that it was time to make architecture more comfortable and appealing to ordinary people, and praised the vernacular buildings that had sprung up without architects' help in the last half of the twentieth century. Commercial development strips and housing strips with their "messy vitality" fall into Venturi's acceptable category: the "Main Street is almost all right" ilk.

Venturi was heralding the arrival of *postmodern architecture* (which was "officially" kicked off by Philip Johnson's design for the AT&T Building in New York, the design of which was released in 1978).

Robert Venturi said of everyman's architecture, "Main Street is almost all right," and designed this fire station in Columbus, Indiana.

1. A stunning young woman holding a glass of Chablis sidles over and murmurs, "I think the work of Venturi is so fascinating!" You respond:

    A. The classicists are the best, aren't they?
    B. I agree. Less *is* a bore!
    C. Sure. Form follows function.
    D. That's just great! You admire a guy who built an ugly house for his mother?

Find the correct answer on p. 175.

2. A neighbor offers you a can of beer, and leaning on your backyard fence, says, "You know, I noticed some small cracks in the cement on my basement wall." You respond:

    A. My god! Call 911!
    B. That's not cement, dummy! It's concrete. Cement is just one ingredient of concrete.
    C. I hope you have "a piece of the rock."
    D. If there aren't stains or water around the cracks, then it's probably no big deal. If they get bigger, though, call a professional.

Find the correct answer on pp. 16–19.

3. At the grand opening of the downtown First National Bank, the bank president gestures to the new shiny red copper roof and says, "I wanted a green copper roof, just like on the old First National Bank! What do you think I should do?" You respond:

    A. There's a sale on green paint at Murray's.
    B. Wait and enjoy the rainbow of colors over the next ten years. After that it will be the green you want.
    C. The best way to go is chemical treatment with sulfides.
    D. Sorry, copper just doesn't turn green as it did in the old days.

Find the correct answer on pp. 37–38.

4. You see some soft gray yuck stuck in between two building panels of a government building. You:

    A. Leave it alone.
    B. Get somebody to push it all the way back into the cracks.

c. Pull it out and throw it away; it's just left over from a sloppy construction crew.
   D. Call the city building inspectors.

Find the correct answer on pp. 42–44.

5. At Whitey's Bar, a big tough bully says, "Jimmy Carter was the closest thing this country ever had to an architect president. He built a treehouse for his kid and now he builds houses for Habitat for Humanity." You respond:

   A. Yes, sir.
   B. Didn't Richard Nixon once build a birdhouse?
   c. Thomas Jefferson designed Monticello and the University of Virginia, you know.
   D. I think you're confusing the work of a contractor with the work of an architect, buddy.

Find the correct answer on pp. 120–121.

6. You find a piece of recently crafted art in your host's living room, and it looks like a bowl of metal spaghetti. Your host says, "What a find, I could have bought it in steel, but for a few bucks more I got this one in commercial wrought iron." You respond:

   A. Nice concept—you must brush your teeth with a magnet.
   B. Great buy—and a durable work of art it is.
   c. You say nothing. You know wrought iron is no longer available commercially, and this guy was bilked.
   D. I prefer cast iron because of its superior workability.

Find the correct answer on pp. 20–22.

7. At a midtown soiree in the penthouse of a seventy-three-story building, you are standing at a window next to an attractive young man who suddenly notices that the building is swaying perceptibly and mentions it to you. You say:

   A. That's just me, making the earth move under your feet.
   B. Jump, quick, it's our only chance!
   c. We're not moving. It's an optical illusion because we're so far from the ground.
   D. Don't worry. Buildings this tall are meant to sway.

Find the correct answer on pp. 72–74.

8. Apparently fascinated by your keen insight, he turns his soft brown eyes to yours and asks, "Is building sway the reason skyscrapers are never more than about a hundred stories tall?" You respond:

A. Yes. And as long as we're standing here swaying anyway, would you care to dance?

B. I'm telling you, this isn't normal. Jump, quick!

C. Building sway is only one problem with very tall buildings. There are also matters such as getting people up and down. And think of the shadow a 200-story building would cast!

D. No, building sway isn't the limiting factor to building height. The sheer weight of the building is. Even on bedrock, a 200-story building would sink and lean like the Tower of Pisa.

Find the correct answer on pp. 169–170.

9. The person at the table next to you at Mamma Maria's restaurant leans over to you and whispers, "Excuse me. Just what is terra cotta?" You respond:

A. It's like chicken tetrazinni—only better!

B. Shhh! We're in an *Italian* restaurant.

C. Who wants to know?

D. It means "baked earth" in Italian. It's that brown stuff the flower-pots on the walls are made of.

Find the correct answer on pp. 6–7.

10. You are sightseeing at Chartres Cathedral. Your traveling companion says, "Wow! Look at those flying buttresses! I wonder why they're there." You respond:

A. You mean those portly gentlemen over there?

B. They hold up the walls from the outside. That lets them have large windows and a high, open interior.

C. The workers climbed up them to build the walls.

D. They're just decoration.

Find the correct answer on pp. 56–57.

11. The architect's credo is:

A. Firmness, commodity, and delight.

B. Liberty, equality, fraternity.

C. I came, I built, I overcharged.

D. Mom, hot dogs, and apple pie.

Find the correct answer on pp. 92–93.

12. You're reading the newspaper about the dangers of radon gas. Concerned, you turn to your companion and say:

    A. Remember to turn off the stove when we leave the house today.

    B. All this nuclear waste from atomic reactors is getting to be a real problem, it says here.

    C. I wonder how well our basement is vented; we could have harmful gases coming out of the foundation.

    D. There's never anything pertinent in the paper anymore. Pass the toast, please.

Find the correct answer on pp. 146–147.

13. At a New York City convention, you're walking through the Jacob Javits center and are struck by its airy openness. "They say this is a space frame; I wonder what that means," your friend says. You respond:

    A. It was the invention of finite-element interactive structural support that allowed us to get into space in the sixties. It really isn't used for buildings that much.

    B. Don't worry about it. It isn't a very efficient use of support materials, and they won't be around much longer.

    C. It's just a new name for an old concept. They've been using space frames forever. That's what holds up the Hagia Sophia cathedral in Istanbul.

    D. A space frame is a three-dimensional support configuration in which large loads are evenly distributed through nodes to web members.

Find the correct answer on pp. 75–76.

14. Later, in a large open warehouse, your friend points to an exposed steel truss holding up the roof and says, "Look at that, they hold up the roof with that long steel bar connected with V-shaped diagonal rods to a bottom bar. The top bar is attached to the columns at either end, but the ends of the bottom bar aren't attached to anything. They're just hanging there. If you're so smart, why is that?" You respond:

    A. The weight of the roof pushes inward on the top bar when it is connected to the columns. The top bar doesn't sag in the middle because force goes through the diagonals and stretches the bottom bar outward, silly.

    B. Trusses come in a variety of lengths, but only one level of strength. This particular building doesn't need to use all of the strength trusses have, so only half of it is attached to the columns, of course.

C. It's poor workmanship. I don't know how the roof is staying up like that, and we'd better leave right now.

D. Architects appreciate the complexity of parallelism and repetition. Although the top bar would suffice alone to hold up the roof, the rest of the truss is added as an industrial decorative element in the international style.

Find the correct answer on pp. 54–55.

15. You're walking across a field and notice a group of boys digging a deep hole. "We'll find buried treasure here if we dig down 20 feet," one says confidently. You respond:

A. You've got a lot of work ahead. You know that the density of dirt increases with every foot. At 20 feet, one shovel full weighs 40 pounds.

B. Remember to slope the sides of your hole outward at least 45 degrees from the bottom edge. You don't want any cave-ins.

C. You kids get out of here. It's against the building codes to dig a hole more than 15 feet deep without a permit.

D. If you had heavy excavation equipment, you'd be able to dig those 20 feet in less than two minutes.

Find the correct answer on pp. 109–111.

16. You're in your office sipping coffee when the office manager comes in with red puffy eyes, a dry throat, and a runny nose, and says, "I've been to the doctor, and she says I don't have a cold or anything. It seems like everyone at work has it, though. What do you think is wrong?" You respond:

A. Maybe there are irritants coming from the air-conditioning vents, out of the carpeting, and in the wall finishes. We'd better look into this right away.

B. It's a symptom of mass hysteria known as sick building syndrome. Everyone here needs therapy.

C. Where did you get that doctor? You need a second opinion.

D. During times of sunspots, especially high levels of ultraviolet light will react with roofing materials, which creates dangerous levels of cyanide gas.

Find the correct answer on pp. 142–143.

17. A real cutie you've been trying to impress for weeks finally talks to you. While you're standing together on a street lined with glass-box buildings, your friend says: "I've been reading that book by Tom Wolfe, *From*

Bauhaus to Our House, and I really think the Bauhaus had a negative effect on our cityscapes, don't you?" You respond:

A. I've read his book, *Look Homeward, Angel*, but I really didn't get much out of it.
B. The Bauhaus wasn't nearly as pernicious as some would assume. I think a lot of people have overblown the Italian influence on our built environment.
C. On the one hand, the minimalist approach to ornamentation doesn't translate well to the American sense of opulence. But I do agree with the importance of attention to detail.
D. Yes. Our cities would be a whole lot better if American architects had ignored the Bauhaus and concentrated on designing stark glass-facade buildings like the ones on this street.

Find the correct answer on pp. 124–125.

18. Your boss walks down the hall shaking his head. "The contractor on our new building says we have to bring in a subcontractor to add fireproofing to the steel structure. I think he's trying to bilk me." You respond:

A. Sounds like he is. What a ridiculous thing to suggest, fireproofing steel.
B. No, he's telling you the truth. Steel actually burns when it reaches the temperatures typical in a large building fire.
C. Chill out. The law requires fireproofing of steel structural elements. If there's a fire, you certainly don't want the steel to weaken and the building to fall down.
D. Call the architects, they'll straighten out that greedy son-of-a-gun.

Find the correct answer on pp. 148–150.

19. Your high-school-age niece says, "I was thinking of majoring in architecture, but there seem to be so few women in that field. Now, why is that?" You respond:

A. Because men are chauvinistic pigs, and they want to hog a good thing for themselves. Do it anyway.
B. Because men are chauvinistic pigs, and they won't admit women have the talent to be architects. Do it anyway.
C. Because men are chauvinistic pigs, and they thwart women's chances to advance to the upper echelons of the profession. Do it anyway.
D. All of the above.

Find the correct answer on pp. 130–132.

20. You are driving your grandmother to visit Aunt Elsie, and your route takes you over a concrete bridge. Granny says, "My, my. The cement on my front walk is always cracking and falling apart. How in heavens does this bridge stay up?" You respond:

  A. They paint it with a coating that holds the cement together.
  B. There are steel rods hidden in the concrete.
  C. It's a special, superstrong concrete.
  D. Can you swim, Granny?

Find the correct answer on pp. 13–15.

Aird, William. The Radical Impact of Telecommunications. *Architecture* (February 1988): 112.

Allen, Edward. 1985. *Fundamentals of Building Construction Materials and Methods.* New York: John Wiley & Sons.

Ambrose, James. 1988. *Building Structures.* New York: John Wiley & Sons.

American Institute of Architects. 1985. *Design for Aging: An Architect's Guide.* Washington, D.C.: The AIA Press.

American National Standards Institute. 1986. *American National Standard Specifications for Buildings and Facilities—Providing Accessibility and Usability for Physically Handicapped People.* ANSI A117.1–1986. New York.

Ashurst, John, and Ashurst, Nicola. 1988. *Practical Building Conservation* series, Vols. 1–5. New York: Halsted Press.

Burchard, John, and Albert Bush-Brown. 1961. *The Architecture of America.* Boston: Little, Brown & Co.

Campbell, Robert. Learning from the Hancock. *Architecture* (March 1988): 68.

Campbell, Robert. A Third Philadelphia Plan: A Critical View. *Architecture* (October 1988): 77.

Cowan, Henry J., and Peter R. Smith. 1988. *The Science and Technology of Building Materials.* New York: Van Nostrand Reinhold.

The Encyclopedia of Architecture. Vols I–V. 1989. New York: John Wiley & Sons.

Franklin, James R. Risk Management: Standard of Reasonable Care. *Architecture* (November 1987): 94.

Geddes, Robert. A Third Philadelphia Plan: The Theoretical Base. *Architecture* (October 1988): 74.

Gordon, Douglas E. Brick Basics. *Architectural Technology* (Fall 1985): 17.

Gordon, Douglas E. Curtain-Wall Connections. *Architectural Technology* (May/June 1986): 33.

Gordon, Douglas E., and M. Stephanie Stubbs. A Global Look at Construction. *Architecture* (September 1987): 103.

Gordon, Douglas E., and M. Stephanie Stubbs. A Potpourri of Other Technological Advances. *Architecture* (March 1987): 82.

Gordon, Douglas E., and M. Stephanie Stubbs. The Rebirth of A Magnificent Monument. *Architecture* (November 1988): 68.

IES Handbook, "Reference" volume. 1986. New York: The Illuminating Engineering Society of North America.

McDonald, Timothy B. Construction of Retaining Walls. *Architecture* (October 1988): 123.

McDonald, Timothy B. Improved Techniques of Superinsulation. *Architecture* (June 1987): 122.

McDonald, Timothy B. Selecting Below-grade Waterproofing. *Architecture* (December 1988): 135.

McLaughlin, Jack. 1988. *Jefferson and Monticello: The Biography of a Building*. New York: Henry Holt.

Osman, Mary E. Highlights of American Architecture 1776–1976. *Architecture* (July 1976): 90.

Perspectives in Vernacular Architecture. 1989. St. Louis: University of Missouri Press.

Rand, George. Indoor Pollution Isn't Going Away. *Architecture* (June 1988): 99.

Salvadori, Mario. 1980. *Why Buildings Stand Up*. New York: McGraw-Hill.

Sawyer, Robert N., and Roger G. Morse. Determining Asbestos Control Needs and Costs. *Architecture* (December 1986): 116.

Stubbs, M. Stephanie. Glued-on Glass. *Architectural Technology* (May/June 1986): 46.

Stubbs, M. Stephanie. Wood Connections: There's a Right Way and a Wrong Way. *Architecture* (December 1986): 111.

Sweet's Selection Data, Sweet's Catalogs. 1985. Chapter SD.5/Wo, Wood/wood properties. New York: McGraw Hill.

Uniform Building Code. 1985. Whittier, Calif.: International Council of Building Officials.

Wilson, Alex. Radon: Testing, Prevention, and Cures. *Architecture* (March 1989): 122.

Wilson, Forrest. Plastics, Past and Future. *Architecture* (April 1988): 103.

Wilson, Forrest. Space Frames, Outer and Inner Space. *Architecture* (September 1987): 110.

Wolfe, Thomas. 1982. *From Bauhaus to Our House*. New York: Farrar, Straus & Giroux.

INDEX